SPIRIT WISDOM

Living Consciously in an
Age of Turmoil and Transformation

An Alexander Book

by Ramón Stevens

PEPPERWOOD PRESS
Ojai, California

Pepperwood Press
Post Office Box 422
Ojai, California 93024
(805) 640-8883

ISBN 0-9639413-9-9

Cover design by Chad Anderson

Printed on recycled, acid-free paper
Printed in the United States of America

for Jamin

with love

Other books by Ramón Stevens

Earthly Cycles: Reincarnation, Karma and Consciousness

Conscious Life: Creating Your Reality

Whatever Happened to Divine Grace?

Contents

Preface

Almost a decade has passed since I felt the first urge to open myself to a consciousness greater than my own, a spirit teacher I call Alexander. Jumping into dictation of his first book only ten days after his introductory greeting, Alexander has since proven to be a prolific, seemingly inexhaustible, source of knowledge.

Alexander dictates his material while I sit in trance before a computer. He takes great care with his prose, choosing words with meticulous precision, rummaging through the word processor's thesaurus, and revising his work before closing each session. The irony, as Alexander describes later, is that he knows nothing of the English language; he feeds his material as pure thought-forms to be translated in my mind.

Wanting to offer Alexander's insights into critical social issues more immediately than the plodding pace of book publishing allows, in 1990 I launched a bimonthly newsletter, *The Alexander Journal*. Each issue offers Alexander's perspective on a topic of cultural or metaphysical interest; subjects have ranged from abortion to dreams, from sexuality to genetic engineering. Alexander has also contributed regularly to *Spirit Speaks* magazine and other publications.

Spirit Wisdom gathers together Alexander's writings from all of these sources, as well as offering previously unpublished and new material. Newsletter essays must often be pruned to fit the *Journal* format; *Spirit Wisdom* restores these commentaries to their original, unabridged length. Alexander has also revised many of the essays, bringing them current with recent events and trends.

Taken together, my hope is that *Spirit Wisdom* will serve as a guidebook to living consciously, illuminating the deeper meanings beneath the critical issues of our time, the better to bring about a socially and ecologically transformed world.

Ramón Stevens
Ojai, California

Introduction

We speak to humanity yet we are not human. We are known by the name Alexander, yet this is a label affixed by our host, Ramón Stevens, to render us comfortably familiar. In truth we are beyond gender, beyond name, beyond human definition. We are spirit, a pool of consciousness beyond the space-time framework of your experience. Yet we carry vital memories of human life, of the struggles and triumphs marking human experience, for within our pool live the soul fragments of hundreds of human incarnations. These blended fragments form a rich treasury from which we draw when addressing ourselves to your personal and collective struggles toward happiness and fulfillment.

One soul fragment was a young widow raising her small children in an age of famine and ceaseless war, whose youngest child sprang from the seed of a brutal passing soldier. From this lifetime we learned tenacity: how an indomitable will, forged in fierce maternal love, stymied death's ceaseless threats to snatch away her beloved brood; and how love conquered even the shame and loathing engendered by the savage genesis of her youngest child.

Another fragment struggled inside the intellectual prison of the Dark Ages, as a brilliant theoretician and experimenter whose investigations threatened the Church's stranglehold on scientific truth. A loner, a lifelong bachelor, he found family and friends a distraction from the volcanic ferment of his mind. From this we learned the thrill of intellectual discovery, of nourishing a mind's insatiable appetite with the fruits of hard-won knowledge, and the intolerable frustration of grinding against a fiercely irrational and repressive authority.

One fragment never lived beyond boyhood, yet his few precious years brought him the experience his soul sought: accepting tenderness, kindness, and sacrifice with grace and dignity. Sickly, weak, mostly confined to bed, the boy appreciated the kindly ministrations of his mother and family even as he refused to fall into self-pity or to debase his dignity with victimhood. Following several lifetimes of haughty, even cruel, positions of power, the boy's soul found its balance in appreciation of loving touch and gentle succor, suffering debility with stoic endurance.

A volatile but loving marriage taught one fragment the value of compromise and the rewards of tenaciously struggling to synthesize two disparate souls into a lasting marital union. Dishes and furniture may have flown, but beneath the daily tumult lay an unshakable commitment to, and respect for, one another. This commitment has served us well, for the husband in that lifetime is now the human host through whom we speak, while the wife remains a vital element of our pool of consciousness. It is through this bond, forged millennia ago, that our present—admittedly unusual—relationship has arisen.

We have long since completed our earthly cycles, the lessons to be gained through animating offshoots of human, animal, and vegetative life. In our present environment we are both student and teacher. We study the larger systems of which human life on planet Earth is but a small fraction; we explore the creation and dynamics of entire universal systems, the one you know and others beyond your imagination. We are a teacher in your realm and others, guiding the denizens of diverse systems to a deeper comprehension of their realities, urging them to transcend the self-imposed limits of their senses and conscious minds; to become active creators of their experience. Our guidance ranges from subtle whispers echoing softly in the dream state to direct, open delivery of lessons in written and verbal form.

We have taken the latter course in your time because the threats to continued viability of the earth's ecosystems are so severe, while fragmentation and implosion of your society intensifies, all leading toward a potentially dark and brutish future—when that future could be so bright. For all your awareness of the breakdown of cultural, familial and ecological systems, few seem to grasp the underlying forces driving the juggernaut of destruction; for as is true in any culture, the deepest, most fundamental values of a society are invisible, beyond questioning for they are never consciously recognized.

Our purpose in delivering the essays contained in this book is to offer this understanding, to help you recognize the deeper beliefs and values which have brought you to this perilous point in your history and to point the way toward a higher consciousness, a more evolved way of thinking and being. Naturally this sounds attractive, but the transition will not be painless for upon the fissured foundation of western culture rest all your comfortably familiar, and ultimately destructive, social systems. Religion, politics, economics, science, education, entertainment—all arise from and reflect the western worldview, a mode of perception and thinking at sharp odds with natural law. All, therefore, must undergo radical transformation if humanity is to survive and prosper in the decades and centuries to come.

We speak with a deep respect for the struggle of being human. It is challenge enough simply to find personal fulfillment and happiness without worrying about the larger world and its travails. Yet you have chosen to participate in the unfolding drama of a world struggling through the death throes of an old culture and birth pangs of a new one, even as that transition makes forging a life of stable comfort still more difficult. We offer our words of guidance in the hope that they assist you, on both individual and collective levels, to ease the transition to a more conscious way of being.

Our blessings on your journey.

Alexander

The Path of
Spiritual and Cultural Evolution

Cultural evolution does not unfold in haphazard, random steps toward a vaguely defined future. Instead, cultures evolve in specific, predictable patterns, reflecting humanity's growing spiritual maturation. The past few decades have witnessed the first steps toward forging a new, more spiritually evolved culture. As you approach the end of the millennium, it will be useful to review these events as a guide toward where you are headed. Let us begin by examining the principles governing humanity's spiritual evolution.

Just as the body's homeostatic mechanisms ensure a steady internal balance and temperature, so is the body of humanity guided by forces which regulate the spiritual soundness of its cultural expressions. When human culture strays from the path of healthy evolution and ventures in directions carrying ominous potential, a process is triggered through which humanity's faltering course can be righted. This process of spiritual realignment has four basic steps.

First, the earth is infused with a sudden wave of spiritual energy, triggering revolutions in politics, art, economics, and especially those areas of human culture manifesting the most egregious divorce from nature and from humanity's spiritual source. This revolutionary thrust shatters the previously inviolate cultural foundation, triggering widespread disillusionment with the status quo, forcing into the open questions long suppressed in cultural amnesia, and threatening the power of institutional guardians. This is an age of chaos and unrest, often playing host to violent clashes between the threatened power structure and advocates for a still undefined new culture.

Following the upheavals and conflicts of the first phase is a second phase of reflection, of rest and introspection, during which the revolutionary turmoil of the first phase cools to a simmer. During this time, the fallout from the revolutionary period is sifted through and evaluated to determine what is truly of value and what should be discarded as the basis for a new cultural worldview. Polarization often arises between those struggling to build a new order and those fighting to maintain the old order.

The third phase witnesses another infusion of spiritual energy, not as powerful as in the first phase, but more specifically focused on empowering those building the new order. That is, energy is slowly drained from the old order while the new order is infused with a fresh energy and power. This triggers an increased polarization between old and new orders, giving rise to hysteria, violence, even madness among advocates of the old order, as their previously steady flow of supportive energy dwindles. This energy is shifted toward those working to bring about a new order in harmony with natural and spiritual principles.

The fourth phase of the process is the "time of trial," the final showdown between old and new orders. During this period, those structures undergirding the old order will collapse at an accelerated rate, provoking even greater hysteria on the part of those who cling still to its crumbling foundation. This is a time of conflict, of potential danger and violence, as humanity must ask itself which course it will choose: maintaining the old order, leading to ultimate collapse of human society and its institutions, or struggling toward the new order, restoring humanity to its neglected spiritual roots.

While this process of spiritual realignment has occurred many times in human history, it manifests now as the events of the past few decades. The Sixties were witness to the first phase, to a sudden infusion of spiritual energy striking at the foundations of western culture, particularly of white male patriarchy. The revolutions in music, film, and literature; the women's, civil rights, and gay movements demanding respect and equal rights for the previously disenfranchised; the flowering environmental movement; fierce protest against the Vietnam War; a generation turning its back on the spiritual barrenness of its parents' culture—all these were trumpet blasts heralding the new order, awaking humanity from its amnesiac slumber.

The Seventies witnessed the second phase, that of reflection and evaluation. Those trends sprouting in the Sixties which carried potential for healthy cultural evolution were more firmly anchored, both in legislation—environmental, women's and minority rights—and in the hearts and minds of the mainstream as it absorbed the impact of that explosive decade. While seemingly less exciting than the tumult of the Sixties, such is precisely the purpose of this second phase, to evaluate the fallout of the first phase and have its salutary trends embraced by the mainstream.

The third phase, the heightened polarization between old and new orders, manifested in the Eighties. This decade witnessed the rise of the right wing in politics and religion, parallel with the increasing strength and numbers of the environmental, New Age, Green, and other "new order" movements. It is important to understand that, for all the apparent strength of the reactionary forces, they represent the dying gasp, the deathbed shudders of the collapsing old order. Their strength is derived from the institutional forces they seek to preserve, despite all evidence that maintaining "business as usual" will only lead to ecological, social, and economic collapse.

An economic system allowing some to accumulate enormous wealth while others live homeless on the street cannot persist. A political system based on the abdication of personal responsibility and the tyranny of the majority cannot be sustained. A religious institution which weaves an anachronistic cosmology of a paternal creator-in-the-sky to which all must pledge obedience or burn in eternal fire cannot answer humanity's spiritual needs. A species which plunders and rapes the planet on which it depends, and whose population grows beyond the planet's capacity to support it, cannot survive. These issues, and more, represent the raw material for the "time of trial" now beginning to unfold in the Nineties.

Two trends are evident: the increased polarization between old and new worldviews, and the rising madness of the old order. As energy is increasingly shifted from the old to the new, the psyches of those clinging to the old order lose flexibility, balance, even the capacity for reason. Because they no longer trust the power of words and argument to restore the world to their vision, they can only lash out in violence. Sinking ever deeper into cells of shared paranoia, they cast themselves as saviors in a battle for control between "world government" and freedom-loving patriots. The danger is enhanced because the old target for paranoid fantasies—communism—has fallen by the wayside, and the government itself has now become the target. For all the horror of the attack on a government building in Oklahoma City, such represents but the opening salvo in a war to be waged by increasingly deranged and violent defenders of the old order.

At the same time, the Nineties are being hailed as the "spiritual decade": books dealing with spiritual themes are massive best sellers, while a "spiritual hunger" is said to afflict the populace. Small wonder: for the stale gruel of the Judeo-Christian tradition cannot speak to the rising waves of spiritual energy uplifting the consciousness of those receptive to a higher way of thinking and being. There must be something more, many feel, something broader, richer, deeper, truer, something to nourish the soul in its hunger for a spiritually grounded way of life.

This is the setup, then, for the time of trial. Society fractures into two increasingly polarized camps: defenders of the old order and embracers of the new order. The question before you is not whether your culture will make the transition —one could no more order the sun not to rise tomorrow morning—but how difficult you will make it, how much damage protectors of the old order will wreak in their struggle against inevitable decline.

A time of trial is also a time of great opportunity. All the pieces are in place to maintain the current social structures and witness unimaginable social and ecological devastation. All the pieces are also in place for creating a new order, one based on ecological restoration, personal freedom, respect for the sanctity of nature, peace and nonviolence, and cultural renewal. Before you lies an age of challenge and opportunity unprecedented in human history—and each individual holds the power and responsibility to decide which vision of the earth's future he or she holds, and to align consciousness and action with manifesting that vision.

The Spiritual Impulse: Mother of All Religion

Every culture's spiritual life differs in dogma, ritual, and celebration, yet all great religions flow from the same fundamental source, interpreted and filtered through each culture's unique lens of time, place, and worldview. Because human consciousness cannot grasp the deepest truths in full totality, each culture weaves its symbolic stories and rites as hints and signs pointing toward the body of spiritual truth which lies beyond the power of word and symbol to express. Just as a song originates in its composer's mind, so can religions be thought of as spiritual music, echoing the richer harmony of their source; and each religion's endurance in time and power to offer moral guidance are determined by its degree of harmony with deeper spiritual truth.

Every human culture has a spiritual element. In some the spiritual is so interwoven with the whole of life that one does damage to the culture by attempting to express its "religion" as distinct from its other cultural aspects. In other cultures, particularly modern western culture, religion is held as a discrete aspect of life, with worship services held at specific times and places while the separation of church from state is inscribed in law.

Everyone has a religion. Everyone carries a philosophical framework or worldview which organizes and gives meaning to life. Even an atheist scientist, convinced that he lives in a random universe devoid of spiritual influence, has a religion: he has faith in the scientific method and in the veracity of the scientific theories spun to explain the world from a purely mechanistic perspective. If a religion's longevity reflects its degree of harmony with the deeper truths, then the mechanistic worldview, several centuries old and collapsing under the ineluctable march of quantum physics, is revealed as grossly disharmonious with the truths which have sustained the world's great religions for millennia and animate them still.

The Universal Truths

What, then, are the fundamental spiritual truths which all religions strive to express? As mentioned, any time a deep truth is reduced to words it necessarily loses its power, becoming a symbolic truth rather than an experienced truth. Nevertheless, enumerating the basic truths in words is a first step on the path toward directly experiencing them.

The first fundamental truth is the essential oneness of creation. This understanding lies at the heart of many great religions. Its paradox is that it directly contradicts the experience of the senses. You see and feel that your body has a distinct boundary at the skin which cleanly separates you from everything else. You see rocks, trees, flowers, buildings, and so on, and affix a different name to each, dividing the world into categories. Each person you meet is unique, and it stretches the mind's limits to imagine that at some level the various races, colors, beliefs and cultures of human experience blend into a unified whole.

Nevertheless, at the deepest levels all is united, all is one. The fantastically variegated phenomenal world is but a thought in the mind of All That Is, whence arise countless other worlds and dimensions beyond your awareness, all flowing from the same source. It is perhaps ironic that western science, heir to a reductionist tradition which splinters and fragments creation rather than perceiving its unity, should offer proof of this most basic truth in the discoveries of modern physics. At the deepest level, one finds no irreducible building blocks of matter, but only waves and fields of vibration; a pulsating, inviolate fabric of energy.

How, then, do you perceive this unbroken field of vibration as discrete objects; what binds your awareness exclusively to your body; why does your mind organize its experience as it does? For this understanding we must turn to a second fundamental truth.

You are consciousness temporarily housed in flesh. While this is understood by many spiritual traditions, western science has inverted the process such that self-awareness is posited as miraculously arising in organisms when they evolve to a certain degree of complexity. How consciousness spontaneously arises from inert matter is never explained; and indeed can never be. For you are consciousness first and foremost, cloaked for a time in physical form. This provides the illusion of separation, of yourself as a discrete being standing apart from the rest of creation.

This is not to impugn the validity of your private experience, nor your uniqueness. Each human life is a unique expression of All That Is, with its private purpose and fulfillment. Just as each of your fingers is unique while embedded in the larger construction of your hand, which in turn is a member of your entire body, so is each human life unique while on deeper terms it unites with all humanity to form a common brotherhood.

Notice that the second truth seems paradoxical at first as well: your senses tell you that you are separate from others while in truth you are one strand in the larger human fabric, itself woven into the whole of creation. Moving beyond the apparent paradoxes is an essential step on the spiritual path.

A third fundamental truth is that the more closely human laws parallel natural laws, the more harmonious and balanced a culture will be. Nature hasn't many laws, but those guiding principles established to maintain balance and harmony in the natural world carry over into human endeavors as well. Because humanity is unique in its free will and highly developed reason, a person or society may choose to follow a path outside of, or to actively violate, natural law. For a while it may appear that one can "get away" with violating nature. Over time, however, the consequence of violating natural law will become apparent.

As an example, one of nature's most fundamental laws is that every action has a consequence. Some religions express this truth as the law of karma; even western science expresses this understanding in the law that every action begets an equal and opposite reaction. For some time humanity has been acting as if it carried special immunity from the consequences of its actions, could plunder and pillage the natural world without ill effect. Now, however, as the ecological crisis demonstrates, the folly and danger of continuously and severely violating natural law become indisputable. To pump oil from the ground and burn it is a violation; to build dams is a violation; to electrify the globe is a violation; to split the atom is a violation; to tinker with genetics is a violation. Each such violation would alone impair the natural world's ability to heal itself, but taken together they threaten a total unraveling of the earth's power to sustain life-supporting processes.

It is no coincidence that such impending catastrophe has been brought about by western science, whose worldview is the first in human history to disavow and disdain spirituality. By refusing to acknowledge any spiritual laws governing human affairs, man is unrestrained by ethics or morals which would temper healthier cultures. The result, the inevitable consequences, can be seen in rain forest destruction, toxic waste, mountains of garbage, degenerative diseases, evaporating ozone, and other symptoms of a planet plummeting toward self-destruction.

The apparent paradox of this third fundamental truth is that humanity's rational mind seems to grant it superiority over the natural world and freedom from natural laws, yet any exercise of reason which violates those laws inevitably redounds to your detriment.

A fourth fundamental truth is that time and space are illusions. This cuts a deeper paradox than merely saying that what your senses perceive is an illusion; for time and space are the very foundation of your experienced reality. Some of the world's spiritual traditions recognize this truth, referring to the illusions of temporal life as "maya," warning against the trap of mistaking sense experience for deepest reality.

Time and space are the two main dimensions into which energy creating temporal events is channeled. Any "event" exists beyond space-time as a grid of energy or intent, eternally viable in all its possible manifestations. Your experience of events is determined by how much "event energy" you draw into your sphere of experience and the balance you strike between expressing the event through time and space. An illness, for example, can be experienced as a minor ache lasting interminably or as a full-bodied crisis quickly healed. The same amount of event energy may be dissipated in both cases, but the space-time balance differs.

Space and time are energy channels, then, through which physically based consciousness experiences events. They have no validity beyond the physical dimension; therefore, in deepest terms, they are illusions. Perhaps no paradox so grates against your waking awareness as this; yet, again, those on the spiritual path must overcome and integrate the paradox, allowing them to live partly in the phenomenal world and partly beyond it.

The Spiritual Impulse

As we mentioned, every human society fashions the fundamental truths into a religious system influenced by its time, place, and culture. The truths are filtered through each culture's prism, refracted into shades of wisdom carrying the energy of their source but not its full vitality.

The unique focus of human life is to express itself through symbol. Language, art, even human relationships, are all symbolic expressions of deep veins of consciousness which bubble to the surface of awareness and seek expression through symbol. You communicate with others through spoken and written language, art, bodily gestures, affection, and violence. You can never fully communicate the condition of your body and the flow of your thoughts at any given time; you selectively filter what you will offer to others as a symbolic summary of your condition.

So it is with the spiritual impulse as it finds expression in the world's great religions, a prayer of grace before a meal, the baptism or initiation of children, or the joy you find in spending time in wild nature. All rites and rituals, symbols and songs, evoke the deeper unspoken spiritual impulse which beats within every human breast, seeking expression through symbol.

What is this spiritual impulse, then? What drives every human culture to fashion schools of thought which explain life's origin and meaning, and offer rules of conduct for proper living?

The spiritual impulse is the hunger for reunion with All That Is, the ultimate source of all creation. Unconsciously knowing that each human soul is a fragment of its greater source, the urge to return to the source, to reunite with it, is the motivating force behind all religious expressions. From the Christian Kingdom of Heaven to the Buddhist nirvana, the religious path always leads the righteous back to the godhead, the source, the creator. The "spiritual path" is thus a trail leading from temporal earthly life to eternal bliss and reunion with creation's ultimate source.

To render the spiritual impulse through art is to grant symbolic expression to the hunger for reunion with the source. To paint a picture, sing a song, or write a book exalting the creator is to forge a relationship with the creator, a bond from the exiled soul to its source. Much of any culture's greatest art is religious in nature for there is no deeper, more passionate inspiration than the longing for reunion with one's spiritual source.

Each human life replicates the spiritual search, whatever the religious beliefs a person holds. For each human life begins by floating in a warm, fluid cocoon of bliss and safety, where all needs are met. Birth is the separation from the source, though newborns do not distinguish between themselves and others at first. Childhood means learning the language, culture, and power to manipulate effectively, all leading toward the day of separation from the parents and embrace of adult responsibilities.

Here a new opportunity for union arises in choosing a life partner, as most cultures favor narrowing the impulse toward union to a single partner with whom one creates a home base of stability and security. The love of a spouse, long-term friendships, and happy community relations all offer "union" to your gregarious species, as human relationships symbolically reflect life's deeper meaning, the search for union with the spiritual source. As each human soul is another fragment of that source, romance and friendship are ultimately the embrace of the creator.

Death, of course, is a profound experience of reunion with the spiritual realm. Many near-death survivors report being bathed in pure white light and being met by deceased loved ones and religious figures. These dramas, enacted in symbolic terms familiar to the still earth-based consciousness, symbolize death's deeper purpose, a release of the ego and sense of separation, an embrace of union with a realm of love and purity.

Consider the religious or spiritual practices which require that one close one's eyes, such as prayer or meditation. This deliberate blocking of sense experience reinforces the sense of turning away from the temporal world and seeking reunion with the spiritual realm. As one grants validity and attention to the spiritual impulse, one naturally seeks to quiet the mind and free the body from sensory excitement, the better to ride the spiritual impulse toward reunion with one's source.

New Spiritual Expressions

Spirituality and human institutions are fundamentally incompatible. While spirituality is intensely private, deeply felt, resonating in each heart with a unique timbre and pitch, human institutions require homogeneity. While spirituality is spontaneous, flowing, and mercurial, human institutions require order, structure, and predictability. While spirituality urges appreciation of and reunion with divine cosmic forces, human institutions are bound to the earth.

Because spirituality and human institutions are incompatible, it follows that any attempt to wrestle spiritual truth into dogma and creed, ceremony and ritual, hierarchy and power, will vitiate the spiritual truth offered by a religion's founder. The founders of the world's great religions opposed the institutions of their day, as true spirituality is liberating and spontaneous, poison to law and order.

In addition, because each culture filters spiritual truth through the prism of its time and place, the great spiritual fires igniting the world's religions dim as time passes and cultures evolve. Words that thrilled Jesus' or Buddha's listeners to trembling and exaltation are read and spoken far more academically in Space Age culture. Thousands of years have passed, cultures have evolved, and the symbolic truths carried in the words of the master teachers, while still noble and inspiring, cannot fully speak to the age in which you live.

The Christian Church has fallen far from its omnipotent power of the Middle Ages. In a culture where the separation of spirituality and government is codified into law, the Church's influence and power are diminished. The Church's structure, a hierarchical patriarchy which until recently forbade women from serving among its leadership, maintains its power and authority by burying the spiritual impulse beneath edifices of ritual and dogma, squelching any hint of genuine mystical experience.

Against such a backdrop, it is inevitable that many would leave the churches in which they were raised, finding them desiccated relics of ages past. The great search for spiritual meaning of the past few decades, particularly the interest in eastern and Native American religions, reflects the unquenchable spiritual impulse seeking fresh expression, free from rigid dogma and respecting the uniqueness of each soul's private experience.

The most recent trend is the rise of interest in "goddess" religions, either ancient or newly devised. The interest in feminine mythological figures, and in seeing the earth as the feminine Gaia, reflects the long suppression of the feminine principle in western religious systems. Christianity and Judaism are male-oriented religions, heavy on structure, form and hierarchy, with women relegated to supporting roles. A healthy culture balances and cherishes both masculine and feminine principles; thus, as western culture struggles to heal its imbalance, the feminine is actively embraced.

The feminine principle is love, forgiveness, compassion, nurturance, gentleness, quiescence, and stability. The earth and nature are often viewed as feminine, rightly so, for these qualities are evident in nature's harmonious web.

The masculine principle derives from the sun's qualities of strength, heat, creation and destruction, randomness, spontaneity, and energy. Western culture is largely based on the masculine principle, particularly with its emphasis on creation and destruction. So the interest in goddess religions, in searching the ancient past for evidence of harmonious cultures which revered the feminine principle and lived by it, reflects the desperate need for balancing, for cherishing and incorporating the feminine principle within western culture's values.

Future Spiritual Expressions

The rising interest in goddess religions is necessary to balance western culture's long emphasis on the masculine principle. But once the balance is restored, once masculine and feminine are equally valued and cherished, how will spirituality evolve? What new spiritual expressions will arise to take the place of traditional religions?

In a sense, every spiritual system is a blend of truth and symbol. Because human consciousness cannot apprehend absolute truth, but must reduce it to manageable fragmentary symbols, every religion is a unique mixture of truth and symbol. The greater the proportion of truth to symbol, the purer the spiritual system is and the longer its endurance and power.

As spirituality evolves, it seeks expression more as truth and less as symbol. It encourages direct experience, direct knowingness of spiritual truth, rather than the absorption of codified dogma. Formalized ritual diminishes as spontaneity and uniqueness are favored as offering more genuine spiritual expression. Hierarchy is replaced with equality, with recognition of the innate divinity burning in every heart, with no penance offered nor salvation sought from outside oneself.

Future spiritual expression is thus likely to be more casual, spontaneous, and democratic. Ceremonies will arise on the spur of the moment, with each contributing whatever he or she feels moved to offer. Most importantly, spirituality will be nature-based rather than god-based. Instead of projecting and worshiping a paternal sky god figure, the earth itself, the expression of the feminine principle, will be honored as the source of life. Ceremonies will be tied to the natural rhythms of season and equinox, and holy water will flow from every spring.

Less symbol and more truth. More natural, spontaneous, original celebrations of the precious gift of life and appreciation for the earth and sun which animate your earthly body. More private introspection, communing with the life force burning inside you; and greater awareness of the spiritual forces which surround and guide you. Most of all, the fundamental truths lying behind all the world's religions will be understood not as words in a book, but as richly felt truths resonating in your heart.

The Ego:
Creator of Your Reality

The ego has been the butt of much scornful derision of late, as if it were an unwelcome intruder insolently hindering your journey toward psychological health, a crude interloper thwarting your smooth ascent to ever greater heights of spiritual purity. The current view is of the ego as a mask, a false face obstructing the true self, hindering the goal of authentic living.

In truth, the ego is as essential an element of your psychological/spiritual being as any other; and human life is impossible without it. It may be the case that in your psychologically troubled culture the ego is blamed for preventing resolution of deep-seated issues, but part of its function is to allow you to navigate through daily life without the weight of the world or your own hurtful past so impinging on your consciousness that you are unable to function.

The ego is a psychological construct mediating between your higher consciousness and physical reality. When you assume physical form, you dip down from the nonphysical realms of oneness and simultaneous time into the three-dimensional realm of symbols and linear time. These two dimensions cannot be synthesized; you cannot live with one foot in each. Thus the ego serves as the portal through which information flows from one dimension to the other, as your higher self feeds its intent for your life into the physical system and your earthly experiences echo up to your higher self.

The ego is the "switchboard" of your greater psychological/ spiritual/physical being. It receives streams of information from your nerves, your senses, your mind, your higher self, those with whom you are telepathically linked, and future events, both private and collective, being pulled toward manifestation. Consider for a moment the condition of your consciousness if all these disparate streams of information suddenly flooded your mind in full intensity: you would be unable to endure the vibrational cacophony, unable to function. The ego's role is to juggle these various information flows, to select which will be emphasized and which placed on "background." The ego paints a smooth, even picture of your daily life even as it balances multiple streams of information, constantly varying their relative intensity as best suits your purpose in each moment.

The conscious mind can absorb only so much at one time. If you think of events as gestalts of energy which are fed into your experience "event unit" by "event unit," like sand trickling through an hourglass neck, then the sum total of all the event units you can perceive simultaneously is held to a certain maximum threshold.

Consider the many common examples of this process. When you want to concentrate your mind's attention on your reading, you turn the stereo or television down (or off) so your conscious mind can "fill" with your reading and be "emptied" of aural stimulation. When you are in severe pain you do not notice a slight stiffness in the joints, for your awareness is flooded with pain which crowds out lesser bodily messages. When you listen to music you particularly enjoy, you turn the volume up so it grips you with peak intensity, suppressing other stimuli. When you experience tremendous and instantaneous pain, shock and horror—as in an automobile accident—you later cannot recall the moment of impact, for the conscious mind was literally overloaded with stimuli and a "gap" in memory marks the moment when the ego's normal functioning broke down.

Given that the conscious mind can absorb only so much at once, it is the ego's job to balance and harmonize the disparate strands of information fed from "below"—the body's sensations and experiences—and "above"—from your mind, higher self, and other discarnate sources—and present you with the picture of a smooth, uniform experience.

The ego functions as a sublime, efficient, and invisible processor of your experience, the creator of your reality. It makes no judgments or decisions of its own volition, but always operates through an established program of instructions which it uses in shaping your experience. Some of these instructions are innate to the entire species, and others are specific to each individual, a unique template of guidelines blending your higher self's intent for your life and your private belief system.

The ego's top priority is to maintain the safety and security of the physical organism. If the body is lost or greatly impaired, so will be all potential for learning and growth in this lifetime. Since the ego's highest "assignment" is to protect the body's integrity above all other considerations, the ego forces a sharp identification with your body as *you*, more so than you identify with your soul or the greater fields of consciousness from which you spring.

The primary source of information as to the body's condition is obviously the body itself, primarily through the senses. Your senses paint a constantly updated picture of where you are, whether your circumstances portend danger or delight, whether you can relax in secure contentment or must bristle with hormonally charged alertness.

Where your safety is assured and danger at bay, the ego can reduce the "bodily integrity" element of your consciousness, allowing other aspects to dominate—such as affectionate play with a child, philosophical discourse, or fixing a meal. When the body senses danger, all other aspects of your being are banished from awareness, flooding your consciousness with the urgent defense of bodily integrity until the danger has passed. Bodily self-preservation is the highest of all instincts.

While the ego receives its primary information on your body's condition from your senses, it receives material from sources beyond the senses as well. The physical body—the *you* you see in the mirror—is wrapped in a cocoon of vibratory fields whose frequencies escape your senses' perception, but which function as the senses do, apprising the ego of environmental conditions.

The first such body is the etheric, a tight glovelike wrapping on the body which sends inquisitive probes into your surroundings, absorbing information escaping the senses. When you feel that someone is staring at you but you cannot see who or where; when you feel nausea while perched on the edge of a cliff—these are the etheric body's messages which the ego tries to funnel into your awareness. Because these messages originate at a vibration above your waking mind's operating frequencies, they must be "stepped down" by the ego and are perceived more as amorphous, diffuse feelings rather than specific information.

The next energetic body is the aura, a swirling cocoon of vibration which carries, in energetic form, information about your physical and emotional condition, residue of the last few days' events, reincarnational and karmic information, your higher self's overall life purpose, and so on. Whenever you come in contact with another individual and the auric fields overlap, this information is exchanged. Your ego blocks conscious awareness of most of this vibratory dialogue because it is not essential to your functioning in the physical world and would betray the freedom and privacy which are your birthrights in the physical system.

Upon meeting another person you may, however, be left with diffuse or even powerful feelings of attraction or repulsion. This indicates either a profound meshing of sympathetic energy fields or the discordant clashing of incompatible energies. In either case, your conscious mind does not receive specific information from the ego as to the reason for the pull or push with this individual, but only a feeling that further interaction would either bring mutual growth or trauma. This is the ego "stepping down" the information absorbed by the aura and feeding it to your conscious mind in diffuse feeling tones.

So the ego has greater sources of information about the body's condition than that provided by the senses and nerves. It receives and processes material gleaned from the higher energy fields surrounding the body and, in cases where that information is of sufficient importance or urgency, messages will be planted in the conscious mind as seemingly inexplicable feelings and hunches.

There is a basic pulsation to the physical system, like a cosmic metronome beating out the pulse upon which all physical life rides. Each person's ego is bound to that basic universal pulse, whose frequency determines both the types of living organisms which may exist in a system and the rapidity with which events play themselves out within it.

As we mentioned earlier, if you consider that events exist essentially as bundles of energy which uncoil and are fed into your experience unit by unit, then the basic frequency pulsation of a given physical system determines how much time is required to fully express and release a given event. The ego, bound to the universal pulse, can process only so many event units with each pulsation. This determines the maximum threshold of information your waking mind can handle at once.

This universal pulsation, since it binds all egos to a common beat, is the basis for agreed-upon systems of time. Your time-keeping mechanisms, if running properly, all agree on what time it is. On a deeper level, your ego shares with all other egos an agreement as to what minute, hour, day, month, year is currently playing out in linear terms, thereby binding the world in a common flow of experience. Because the ego is the nexus binding physical reality with the nonphysical dimensions, where time does not exist, it is crucial that all living organisms in a system ride upon a common frequency.

The ego is the intersection point between the infinite fields of probable events swarming in timeless vitality and the bedrock physical system of linear time. Beyond the physical system, all events hover in simultaneous perpetuity. When you draw certain probable strands into your life, the ego processes those events by feeding them into waking awareness one unit or several units at a time until each event is released. Riding atop the universal pulsation, the ego oversees the flow of the many simultaneously unfolding events of your life, weaving them together into the illusion of a seamless tapestry of experience.

The intensity of your experience of each event is determined by how many event units the ego feeds into expression with a given pulsation. This judgment is made based on the nature of all other events simultaneously occurring at the time and their relative importance. Many events are eminently plastic in their temporal duration, and your free will dictates how quickly or slowly they play out. When you scream and gnash your teeth in reaction to loss of a loved one, you release the "event" of grieving much more quickly than if you keep a stiff upper lip, mourn quietly for years, and develop an ulcer as an icon of your suffering.

The ego does not simply process events occurring in the "now" moment, but carries awareness of events as they approach manifestation, before the first event unit is fed into your experience. Because you magnetically attract each event of your life out of the swarms of probable potential hovering around you, and because that attraction reflects the nature of your beliefs and thoughts, the ego can often surmise with sharp accuracy which precise probable events you will pull into manifestation. It therefore knows ahead of time which events it will be processing, their overall intensity, and your likely reactions to them.

As a result, the ego can prepare the body for impending events by altering its chemistry. For instance, if injury is anticipated the immune system can be kicked into high gear in anticipation. With its primary mission being the integrity of the body, the ego anticipates the impact of future events and prepares the body beforehand to cushion any potential blows to its integrity.

We mentioned that your beliefs and thoughts largely determine the nature of your experience. You create your reality through your beliefs and thoughts, for these carry an electromagnetic reality within the brain and nervous system. As probable events approach your experience in their infinite potential, the probable "slice" you experience is pulled into manifestation by the electromagnetic swirl generated by your beliefs. The ego's job is not to pass judgment on the events you pull into experience, not to block those you might consider unpleasant, but to grant you the freedom and responsibility of reaping the events you have sown in your thoughts.

Of course there are other, greater influences on your life's experience besides your thoughts and beliefs. Your higher self, when it formed your life's germinal potential, did so with a specific life challenge in mind, a certain theme weaving itself through your journey from birth to death. At the very least, this "tuning" of your life experience makes certain events more likely than others. More important, it grants you relative freedom from trouble in some areas while focusing your attention on those areas where progress seems to come so slowly and with much struggle.

The ego stands as the intermediary between these two great influences on your life's experience, your higher self's intent for your life and the belief system you develop from birth onward. It may be the higher self's intention that you experience a certain event at a certain time in your life. As that probable event moves toward manifestation, the ego looks to your thoughts and beliefs to determine how "intense" a potential slice to feed into your life. Thus it is crucial to understand that *your beliefs are the ultimate creator of your experience*. Whatever the higher self's intent, your ego gives greatest weight to the dynamic, ever-changing flow of your thoughts. In this way your absolute freedom and ultimate responsibility are ensured.

The same holds true for events arising from reincarnational or karmic origin. Almost every life carries as part of its overall challenges one or more karmic relationships to be worked on—and, hopefully, resolved—thus cleaning up your soul's blemishes in preparation for ultimate release of the earthly dimension.

Karmic influences are usually fed into your life's stream as *themes* rather than specific events. If you murdered someone in a past life, it does not follow that he must murder you to balance the relationship. You and your past victim could devise infinite scenarios through which this wound could be healed. Again, the ego looks to your thought patterns to determine which probable events could be pulled into manifestation that would serve the purpose of releasing the karmic bond while reflecting your state of mind. In this case, the two participants would have to agree on a given course of action that synthesizes both life purposes and both belief systems. This agreement would most often be worked out in the dream state, then fed to the two egos to craft events of mutual benefit.

❖   ❖   ❖

The ego is often disparaged for its narrow focus, for emphasizing the primacy of the body to which it is attached and in so doing losing the larger picture, the great commonality binding the great human family. In addition, the ego seems to possess an unlimited repertoire of diversionary tactics preventing perception and resolution of deep psychological trauma, allowing you to move past the hurts of childhood to a stable, fulfilling adulthood.

It is important to recognize that these attributes of the ego are not universal, but reflect its adaptation to the skewed ideas and worldview of western culture. At the very root of your culture lies its core value of *separation*, and upon this foundation are built your scientific, religious, and political systems. Founding a culture on the value of separation produces an individualistic society in which each person must be afraid for his or her health, shelter, food, and financial security. No matter how wealthy your neighbors or family members may be, you alone are responsible for yourself, and failure can mean freezing to death on the streets.

In such a system, the ego's normally smooth, invisible functioning is corrupted into maintaining a low-grade panic at all times. In a system where there is never enough to go around, one must worry constantly about financial stability, the source of adequate food and shelter. Since the ego's top priority is protection of the body's integrity, and the body is threatened by living in a system where food and shelter are in no way guaranteed, the ego rides on a constant cloud of fear.

Since the mind can handle only so much information at once, this constant low-grade panic crowds out and diminishes life's other possibilities. And because concern for the body is its top priority, the ego resists the kind of introspective probing that is essential to psychotherapeutic understanding and healing. It is too much for the ego to maintain its low-grade fear and simultaneously exhume childhood trauma. So the ego masks childhood pain with a wealth of diversions—

projection, compensation, transference, and blissful amnesia—anything but having to fully face and process deep psychological wounds.

Of course, those wounds arise from a culture based on separation, where each generation of fractured souls turns around and cripples its children. Yet the struggle to achieve psychological health is hampered by the ego's concern for the body's security; and in a vicious cycle the unresolved trauma one experiences in childhood, one often visits on one's own children.

Thus the ego's normal functioning is tainted in your culture, for it *interferes* with your free will rather than enhancing it. It has no choice, given its highest priority of protecting bodily integrity, living in a culture which casts off unwanted and "unproductive" men, women, and children like old newspapers. Every time you pass a beggar on the street your ego shudders, for it knows that there but for the grace of God go you. And in its sharp focus on corporal security, its low-grade panic diminishes your potential experience in every other area of life.

Thus the disparaging attitude toward the ego is misplaced. In a healthy culture, the ego makes no judgments, forms no opinions, would never presume to splinter reality into broken fragments as your culture does. It is in the mind that each culture's conceptual framework is passed from generation to generation. If your culture now faces stark reminders of its separatist, alienated worldview in the growing ranks of the despairing homeless, the fault lies not with the ego but with your culture's beliefs and values, with which the ego is forced to contend at the cost of its normally invisible functioning.

The ego's job is neutral, a dispassionate switchboard drawing in huge swarms of information from sources as diverse as your past lives and your cold toes, weaving these disparate threads into a cohesive, coherent life tapestry. It is the funnel through which your higher self pours its intent for your life into your body. It is the preserver and protector of that body, whose alert protection never wanes for an instant in all your decades. It is the "I" binding body to spirit in a unique life journey.

Because the ego's top priority is maintaining the body's security, when physical life is released the ego largely vanishes with it. The sharp identification of "me" versus "not me" melts into a swarm of consciousness in which such sharp demarcations are released in favor of building ever greater gestalts of consciousness free of personal identity. Yet as long as you remain in physical form, your ego is your guide, protector, creator of your experience—the mark and meaning of that unique bundle of divine potential you call "I."

The Many Faces of You:
Probable and Multiple Selves

One of the most difficult concepts for students of meta-physics to grasp is probabilities. Stated briefly, while you conduct your life in the apparent security of a consistent reality and stake your claim to one historical and biographical life history, all about you swarm unseen versions of yourself, probable versions of yourself, which play out in full vitality those paths you have not taken. Every time you face a choice, a two-path decision, whichever path you do not consciously choose to follow will indeed be pursued by another "you," a probable "you."

This makes answering the age-old question "Who am I?" considerably more complex. The question might be better stated, "Who are we and why are we running around the cosmos like beheaded chickens?" Further, is the *you* reading these words somehow more valid, more real, than the many probable yous who have never picked up *Spirit Wisdom*? To these questions we address this chapter.

The Soul's Freedom

The universe's design grants infinite freedom through its play of probabilities. Each spark of intent beaming from a higher self into earthly existence enters a system built not on only one historical earth and one narrow path for you to tread, but splashes into an infinite sea of potential. Just as each of you carries multiple probable selves throughout life, so are there probable earths, probable histories, playing out in full richness and vitality outside the scope of your senses.

The soul's freedom is to select which probable history it wishes to serve as background prior to physical birth, to narrow the focus onto a small probable slice of family history as clan background, and so on. Your "higher self," the cohesive, undifferentiated bank of intent from which your probable selves spring, can choose among many such historical and family backgrounds, the better to provide a rich variety of experience. Imagine how different your life would be if, given the same personality, intelligence, and talents, you were raised in an orphanage, a castle, a ghetto, a farm. By sending shoots of intent into various probable versions of earth's history, a higher self gains this rich breadth of experience.

No probable version of your life is more valid than any other. There is no "primary consciousness" which swims among probable versions of your life while the others serve as ghostly background. Each probable self is as vital, as conscious, as *real* as you are. To understand how this can possibly be, how there could be multiple versions of yourself living out vastly different lives utterly unknown to you, we turn now to the electromagnetic construction of the physical system and the psyche.

The Body and Soul Electric

The physical system is organized and maintained according to the laws of electromagnetism. Electromagnetism, in turn, reflects deeper natural laws which govern both physical and nonphysical systems.

Very briefly, the laws of electromagnetism govern the interaction of particles of matter, organize them into patterns of increasing complexity, determine the temporal duration of objects, and provide the informational feedback loops essential for animate life to come to form. Imagine a sea of swarming electrical sparks teeming throughout the universe, whose immense elasticity and potential for organizing into complex form grant physical expression to the bodies of consciousness seeking experience of material life.

Probabilities arise by organizing this immense electromagnetic swarm into multiple systems, each tied to a unique "core vibration." A core vibration has both a distinct frequency and a unique pattern, or shape to that frequency, which serves as the unifying vibration of a given system. If the universe is music, then every probable universe carries a specific note as its fundamental tone; more, just as the same note played on a piano, violin, or trumpet will color the note with resonance unique to the instrument, so is the fundamental tone or frequency of a probable system colored to differentiate it from others.

Each probable universe carries a unique core vibration which provides the fundamental vibrational tone to all structures, animate and inanimate, within a given system. This core vibration "locks" you into your probable system for life, narrows the potential field of experience, and provides a bedrock consistency undergirding your life's events.

Human consciousness contributes the "rational" focus to the stew of animate form; humanity is the master manipulator, creator, destroyer, artist, empire builder. To progress technologically, you depend on certain physical laws to always be true, you require substances to interact in predictable ways, you need the security of experimental repeatability, like causes rendering like effects. Imagine a world in which one day molten iron rendered steel, the next day it rendered gold, the next day it rendered soap. You would be unable to progress technologically for the security of predictability would be lost.

Because the "laws of nature" you hold to be immutable truths are truths *only within your probable system*, and carry little or no validity in other systems, you must narrow your focus to one probable universe with its unique set of "laws" governing the organization and interaction of matter, and remain firmly ensconced within your chosen system. This is ensured by harmonizing your body's core vibration with the core vibration of the probable system your higher self has chosen to explore. This locks you into your system and blocks from awareness the life activities of your other probable selves in their distinct realities.

The variety of probable systems spreads out along a continuum, with immediately adjacent systems operating under laws virtually identical to yours; were you to slip into an adjacent system, no great shock would await you, no through-the-looking-glass Wonderland would confound you with its clearly impossible workings. The farther away on the continuum you move from your own system, however, the less your "laws" apply and the more matter is organized and behaves differently.

As an example of one of the infinite gradations of "natural law" available to your higher self, you know that consciousness holds a certain influence over matter: advanced meditators can will their heart rate to slow, the placebo effect brings relief from pain with no genuine pharmaceutical intervention, and so forth. Thus the "mind-matter" influence is valid in your system to a certain degree, though the power of mind over matter seems tenuous and not at all consistently verifiable.

Moving to the extremes of the continuum in this respect, at one end are probable realities where matter is far more receptive to consciousness than to physical laws, and objects readily move simply by wishing them to move. At the other end of the spectrum, the pull of matter binding to itself, impervious to influence by consciousness, is so strong that not even the most enlightened avatar could will his heart to slow; indeed, only with great effort could one override the body's involuntary breathing pattern, which in your system is eminently under your control.

Another continuum binding probable systems is the relative flexibility of consciousness, its ability to consider new information in light of old models of reality and to adjust accordingly. The pattern in your system is for a new idea offered by an avatar or artist to meet with initial scorn and rejection, then gradually to attract adherents, and, after a period of years or decades, to find mainstream acceptance. Thus your system plays host to a blend of progression and retrogression, with the mainstream gradually evolving toward higher states of thinking.

Consider the issue of slavery, how long it took from the first spark of out rage at the obscenity of selling human beings until the Emancipation Proclamation was signed, and even now how many carry lingering hatred and disdain for the formerly enslaved race. On one end of this probable continuum, where consciousness operates more flexibly, one person speaking out against slavery would trigger an instant epiphany among the mainstream, an immediate discarding of an inhumane system, and a more evolved social condition would rapidly be created. On the other end of the spectrum, where consciousness clings to old models more tenaciously than in your system, far more centuries would be required from the first spark of outrage until the dismantling of the slavery system.

You see, then, that the parameters of your system you take for granted—that mind exerts a certain influence over the body and matter, that social progress occurs through a process of long and heated debate—are not immutable verities, but are relative values of your system, positions staked out along the infinite continuum of probabilities. The purpose, again, is to offer the higher self and higher self as rich and varied an experience of earthly life as possible. By sprinkling probable "yous" along the continuum, you enhance your experience, seeing it from all angles: the mainstream political liberal, the intractable racist, the enlightened avatar.

You feel the traces of your probable selves every day, hear their echoes in your inner thoughts. Some days your love of humanity knows no bounds, others you loathe your fellows with misanthropic fury; most days you bob somewhere between these extremes. While you remain ensconced within your chosen probability, you are bound to all probable versions of yourself by the slender strands of consciousness leading to your higher self, and here you are apprised of the condition of your fellow travelers' many life paths.

By harmonizing your body's core vibration with a certain probable system, you narrow your focus to a specific point on the continuum through which each probable self will play out its life. The purpose, you can see, is to offer your higher self the widest possible experience while respecting that human consciousness requires the security of predictable physical laws on which to build its cultural and technological innovation.

It is essential to understand that the matter in each probable system can interact only with matter in its own system. Only particles bearing an identical core vibration can recognize or influence each other. The seeming impossibility of infinite probable earths occupying the same space as yours is no more impossible than having multiple channels available on your television or radio, while you can tune in only one channel at a time. Every day you stroll through boulders, walk on water, soar through the clouds of other realities, while your earth is visited by beings your senses cannot detect. Only the version of earth sharing the core vibration of your body will be available to your senses; everything else—the swarming infinite sea of potential—passes through you undetected.

Multiple Personalities

If the model we have sketched above is difficult to grasp, let us now complicate it considerably by discussing the interplay of probable selves within each narrow probable system. Not only does your higher self have infinite freedom to shoot projections of intent to life among the various probable earths, but each such shoot of intent—springing to life as one human life span—carries with it infinite possibilities for how its life will play out. Each incarnated soul carries a specific life purpose, a theme to be played out on the earthly stage, but as with any work of art this theme can be expressed in countless ways.

If you consider your own past for a moment, perhaps you can see trends and events which seem to provide the foundational theme for your life. This theme will crop up repeatedly in various guises, whether through health, relationship, economic, parent-child or artistic challenges, to name a few. Outside this central theme, your life will not be as beset with difficulty; other aspects will flow more smoothly. These areas of stability provide the sturdy foundation for your life's primary theme or challenge.

Now, this theme can play itself out in infinite ways. Whatever the fear that blocks your fullest happiness—and challenges are almost always expressed through fears, of happiness, success, intimacy, rejection, and so on—you carry potential for both triumphant conquering of that fear and miserable entrapment by it. Between these two extremes lie infinite gradations, of course. Your challenge is to work through the fear, to release its grip on your soul.

Whatever your central life theme is, most often expressed through a specific fear, your higher self creates as many different outcomes of the challenge as one lifetime can carry. If you fear rejection, for instance, you could stagger from romance to romance, always behaving so badly that your partner is forced to reject you; you could cloister yourself as a celibate monk (real or figurative) and refuse to face and resolve the fear; you could struggle to under stand your first few failed romances and resolve to change your outlook and behavior so you no longer invite rejection, even triumphing in the bliss of long-term relationship. Every potential outcome of a given life challenge will be built into the soul at birth, granting un- limited freedom to your conscious will as to how your chal- lenge will be resolved.

Because all such probable selves carry an identical core vibration, they do not spread themselves out along the vibra- tional continuum, living out their lives in realities foreign to your own. Rather, the probable variations on one specific self create a cluster of potential, riding the same probable track from birth to death. These potentials accompany you like ghostly companions, shadows of the future. To differentiate them from the probable selves living in different vibrational realities, we will call these probable variations on a single life- time "multiple selves."

Each multiple self lives out its life in full richness and vitality, yet from the perspective of each multiple self its brethren multiple selves are like dreams, rich with meaning yet somehow unreal. Each multiple self carries a different in- tensity to the core fear or life challenge to be worked through in a lifetime.

We cannot delve at length into the nature of events and how they are pulled into expression, but any "event" is a bun- dle of electromagnetic potential carrying a specific frequency and pattern. Your core vibration and the pattern of your thoughts link with those events most in harmony with their vibrational qualities, so you quite literally create the events of your life through the blend of core vibration and thought pat- terns. Each multiple self is tuned to attract events with great- est ease somewhere along the continuum between triumphant conquering of fear and paralyzed surrender to it.

To continue our example, if the core fear is of rejection, then one multiple self will be tuned to attract "rejection events" of a mild nature, easily overcome; another will be tuned to attract rejection more easily and frequently, requiring greater effort to conquer; yet another will be tuned so strongly toward powerful, life-shattering rejections that successful resolution of the fear can come only through the deepest inner work and lifelong effort.

Because you share an identical core vibration with your multiple selves, you can swim among them with the greatest ease. Indeed, you do this all the time; and at critical "portals" throughout your life have switched tracks, either as a result of having resolved a major challenge or having surrendered your broken spirit to it.

When you become a new multiple self, the vibrational matrix of your psyche naturally changes and its degree of congruence with the matrices of others will be affected. You find old friends and family members falling away, those unable to join you in your life's new journey, while other friends and family members become closer because you have now become a multiple self in greater harmony with *their* patterns. Like attracts like.

If the change was so radical that no connecting strands remained to bind you to old friends and family, death might well be chosen *in your old probable reality* just so you could "cut the ties" completely; you would then live out the rest of your life in a fundamentally different reality, building a new circle of friends and family. The determinant is whether you make a minor shift or a major shift. With a minor shift, you merely collect a new circle of friends; with a major shift, you may have to literally "die" to your old friends to get them to release you from their thoughts, enabling you to embrace an accelerated life.

Perhaps you can look back on your life and identify the portals, points at which major decisions were made which forever changed the course of your life. Some portals' timing is culturally imposed, such as leaving home or choice of a college. Others, while fulfilling cultural expectations, are left to individual choice, such as choice of a job or choice of a spouse. Still other portals open up unexpectedly, either as sudden crisis or sudden opportunity, and here is where multiple selves swarm into awareness, offering their various potentials. At such "portal points" the transition from one multiple self to another is easiest, for growth has somehow become hindered in your life's path, and a portal crisis or portal opportunity opens up to stimulate heightened awareness of and accelerated progress toward resolution of your life's chosen theme.

While riding atop the same core vibration, multiple selves are tuned to experience your life's chosen theme with varying degrees of ease or difficulty in achieving happy resolution of that challenge. Because the intrinsic "tuning" of each multiple self attracts events in harmony with its vibration, perhaps you realize the importance your thoughts and beliefs play in attracting future events to you. Indeed, while many can resolve their life challenges happily without consciously working on "retuning" their psyches, understanding and implementing a program of deliberate retuning greatly accelerates the progress toward such resolution.

The Mental Tune-Up

If your core vibration is implanted at birth and remains constant, save a shattering burst of enlightenment, your power to alter the nature of events you attract to yourself lies in the other major determinant of those events, the vibrational matrix of your thoughts and beliefs. Here is where you can retune the magnetic attraction to life events, shift your position on the continuum away from "negative" events and toward "positive" results.

In truth, you are not so much altering your thought patterns as you are *deliberately opening a portal through which you ride to become another multiple self.* The self that is you now, today, will continue to play out its drama at your current level of event patterns, while you switch your consciousness into a multiple self whose burden is lighter. This is not as esoteric or bizarre as it sounds for, as we have mentioned, you have swum through a number of multiple selves on your path to who you are today. We wish to emphasize that the process need not be entirely unconscious; there are tools to accelerate your growth toward higher states of being.

The primary tool for such work is affirmation. A consistent, daily program of affirmation retunes the nature of your thoughts, elevates them to a higher psychic atmosphere where you attract fewer negative theme-events to yourself, and when they do manifest you resolve them more consciously and easily. You are pulling yourself along the life-theme continuum, you see, deliberately rewiring your mental processes so your life theme finds less onerous expression.

Another commonly used tool for creating life events is visualization, where a specific desired event or object is burned into your mental screen as instruction to the psyche to manifest the object of desire. While it can be highly effective, visualization *will not work* unless the mental retuning described above has been accomplished. Events can manifest only where a psyche of congruent vibrational pattern attracts them to expression. The groundwork must be laid first, the psyche's vibrational matrix accelerated to allow manifestation of the visualized event.

A detailed discussion of how to design an affirmation and visualization program is beyond the scope of this essay. Our point is that the process of swimming through multiple selves need not be unconscious; through a consistent program of affirmation and visualization, your progress toward easing the burden of your life-theme and resolving it happily can be accelerated.

Cosmic Freedom of Choice

We offer a worldview knowing no fatalism, determinism, or random chance. At every step, free choice informs the process. Your higher self chose to experience earthly life in your historical period. It created probable variations of your life path along the many continua, the many versions of earth's progress, spread before it in infinite potential. And you play out one lifetime on one probable earth, while your multiple selves swarm around you like dream counterparts, offering a private continuum along which you play out your chosen life task. Even here, even swimming among this infinite potential and freedom, you carry the power to transform your life into a version offering greater happiness and peace, for the price of five minutes a day in quiet affirmation.

The play of probabilities and multiple selves thus fulfills two purposes: It offers your higher self the richly complete experience of a given theme played out in every probable variation; and it ensures your freedom by surrounding you with multiple-self companions, each playing out a unique version of your life challenge, and among which you freely swim, sculpting the life of your choosing as you strive toward the ultimate happiness lying in vibrant potential before you.

AIDS and Ecological Crisis:
Human and Global
Immune System Breakdown

Orthodox medicine views AIDS as a condition caused by a virus which weakens the immune system of its host. Research into potential cures for the disease therefore focuses on drugs to kill the virus and vaccines which would protect the uninfected from being ravaged by the disease should they become infected. These research approaches are natural expressions of western medicine's view of the body as a machine prone to invasion by hostile outside organisms, the defense being to destroy the invaders or render them harmless within the body with a preemptory vaccination attack.

Let us look at AIDS from a new perspective, a larger holistic perspective.

Nature as an Organism Chain

You are accustomed to viewing yourselves and the elements of nature as discrete entities divided into species, genus, phylum, and so forth, all increasing in specialization and differentiation. As a machine has parts, so does nature have its "parts" which work together to create the larger ecosystems, local and global, sustaining life on earth.

We propose another way of looking at nature. We propose that each element—from the electron to the butterfly to the solar system—is an organism embedded within a larger organism, which in turn is embedded within an organism of even greater complexity, and this "organism hierarchy" grows to encompass the whole of the universe.

Each element of creation exists both as a discrete entity in itself and as a constituent of a larger structure. An electron may be thought of as a precise focus of charge, but has no meaning outside the larger atomic structure of which it plays a part. A cell of your body has a clearly defined cell wall separating it from its neighbors, yet such a cell floating in empty space would have no life or meaning: its meaning arises from contributing to the structure and health of your body.

While examples on these levels are obvious, the relationship of each individual entity to the larger structure to which it contributes, and which in turn gives the individual meaning, holds true on all higher levels as well. Each member of a given species—a bird, a fish, a person—is both an independent individual and a member of a larger "organism," the species to which it belongs. While species vary greatly in their proclivities toward tribal activity versus solitude, the need for procreation compels even the most solitary of creatures to associate with others of their species, surrendering their isolation to participate in the perpetuation of the larger organism, the species.

Consider the aftermath of a major natural disaster occurring anywhere in the world. The media—nerve fibers of the human organism—broadcast the news worldwide; the details are absorbed avidly and with great concern by persons with no personal stake in the disaster, knowing no one involved. At such times, even political and religious animosities are set aside as the species acts as a single organism to bring relief to the afflicted. Money, food, and medical supplies are directed toward the site from around the world to quicken the healing.

Consider how similar this process is to your body's reaction to the "natural disaster" of injury or broken skin: all resources are mobilized and focused on healing the wound. White blood cells swarm to the site, blood coagulates into

protective scabs, and the body sets aside its normal functioning to focus on healing the wound. Depending on the injury's
severity, shock or coma ensures that the body is immobilized
until its all-important healing process is established.

Just as the cells of your body sacrifice their energy or lives
to sustain the larger organism of which they are a part, just as
human beings send compassion and supplies to political ene-
mies in time of natural disaster, so are all species part of a still
larger organism granting them life and meaning: the earth
itself. Because of its size, and because of the limits of human
consciousness, the earth has long been viewed as a sphere of
rock floating through empty space. Applying the "organism"
perspective, however, we see that the earth is one element,
one independent entity, embedded in the larger organism of
the solar system, which in turn is part of a galaxy, and so on.

While it may at first appear difficult to conceive of the
solar system as an organism, given the vast spaces between its
constituent parts, the atoms comprising your body have the
very same structure: scattered agglomerations of mass sus-
pended in a vast empty space. The atom and the solar system
have the same basic structure, then, but are simply organisms
of different size.

At each level of organism structure, the consciousness of
an organism focuses primarily on two levels: most intensely at
the level of the individual, being aware of itself, and then on
the larger organism of which it is a part. The cells of your
body know themselves most intimately and recognize, after
their own fashion, that they play a part in sustaining a larger
organism, your body. Similarly, each of you is most intimately
aware of yourself, and yet your consciousness also broadens
to encompass the next level of organism structure, the human
species—your family, friends, community, world—as your
source of meaning and purpose.

Consciousness, then, is generally limited to an individual's awareness of itself and the larger entity of which it is a

part; it does not normally "step down" to those smaller elements comprising the individual. You are not aware of the lives and deaths of your body's cells; you do not sense their communication; you are not swept up in the drama of healing a wound; you can only observe the overall results with detachment. You do not "care" about the individual cells in your body, just as they do not "care" about the atoms which comprise them.

Gaia: A Living Organism

The earth is simply one level of complexity in the universal organism, a gradation between the smaller levels of species and physical elements, and the larger level of the solar system. This intuitive awareness emerges now as earth is granted a name, Gaia, and is credited with the attributes of life and consciousness. This is a crucial step, for it indicates that the human species is expanding its awareness beyond the immediate levels of individual/species to embrace the still larger planetary organism. Human consciousness stretches to embrace and comprehend the magnificent complexity of the host organism which gives it life and meaning.

The Electromagnetic Basis of Life

All life—all elements of the physical system—is created, sustained, and governed by the laws of electromagnetism. "Electro" refers to the pulsing spark immanent in all matter, while "magnetism" refers to the push-and-pull of attraction and resistance which governs the interaction of matter. As consciousness seeds the physical world from beyond the space-time dimension, it uses the principles and properties of electromagnetism as the medium through which it finds expression.

The basic form of any living organism is a dense agglomeration of matter, what you perceive with your senses as the body, and swirling fields of electromagnetic energy which envelop the body in a roughly spherical pattern. These fields are not detected by the normal five senses. They exist at a higher frequency than the senses are designed to perceive.

An organism defines itself and bases its self-awareness on its body. The surrounding fields of energy and vibration, while bound to the body, stretch and expand beyond it, serving as the link to the larger organism of which one is a part. For example, when speaking to someone standing two feet away from you, your senses perceive that you and she are two quite separate and distinct bodies separated by empty space. From the energetic perspective, however, your two energy fields overlap and mingle, creating a hybrid energy field and essentially linking both bodies into a third "organism" which blends the two energy fields and transmits information on frequencies not perceived by normal consciousness. This linking is the basis for the larger species organism, the human organism, through which all persons are literally connected to each other.

Just as all members of a given species are linked together by invisible fields of energy, so does each organismic level communicate with those above and below it. A perpetual flow of information courses from the highest levels to the lowest levels and back up again.

If enough of your body's cells are in distress, eventually you will feel an ache, a signal that a portion of your body is suffering. While communication across organism lines lacks the intensity binding members of a given organism, still this flow of information keeps each level of the universal organism apprised of the condition of every other level.

Human Interference with Global Health

The earth, like every organism, is a dense body of matter surrounded by electromagnetic fields which are essential to its health and communication with other levels of the universal organism. While orthodox science views the earth as spinning in space, passively absorbing radiation from the sun, in truth the earth's electromagnetic field apprises it of disturbances in the sun's radiation, allowing the earth to alter its atmosphere so as to minimize disturbance to terrestrial and oceanic life. The earth's electromagnetic field acts as a sensor—just as your swirling field of energy acts for your body—informing it of fluctuations in the stream of solar radiation and allowing it to take protective action.

Much is made these days of the severe ecological degradation the human species has wreaked upon the earth. Hints of disturbance in the earth's protective atmosphere, such as gaps in the ozone layer over the polar regions or global warning, serve as alarms that the planet's overall health is threatened, yet these findings are but the surface level of a far deeper, more insidious and ominous development: the electrification of the earth.

Little thought is given to the consequences of stringing power lines across the continents and under the oceans, of filling the electromagnetic spectrum with radio and television signals, of the power plants generating electricity to light the world. Little thought is given because so little is known of the earth's electromagnetic field and its role in sustaining surface life. Every ecological problem must be subsumed under the profoundest threat to life on earth: the proliferation of man-made electromagnetic fields which blanket the earth.

The earth's electromagnetic field, on which it depends to apprise itself of universal conditions and to protect itself and its creatures, is literally being destroyed. If you were placed in a room and bombarded with ear-shattering music, blinded by flashing lights, while your skin was jabbed with needles, how well could you function? That is the condition in which the human species has now placed the earth.

Human and Global Immune System Breakdown

As every level of organismic structure bears similarities in form to other levels, with complexity increasing with the size of the organism, so are there parallels between the global and human immune systems. In the human body, as you know, the immune system destroys invading foreign agents and incipient cancers within the body. Its focus, therefore, encompasses the world beyond the body itself, as it must recognize a "foreign" agent from a cell of its own body, must know to differentiate between the two. The existence of the immune system at all is the body's recognition of a world outside itself and its potential for influence—good or ill—on the body's health and integrity.

Thus the human immune system is a cruder physical version of the electromagnetic field surrounding the body. The body's electromagnetic field senses environmental conditions above the range of vibration perceived by the senses, while the immune system is focused at the physical level, on the body's cells and on foreign agents invading the body.

As mentioned above, the earth has a similar structure. It has an electromagnetic field, roughly overlapping the atmosphere, which senses the streams of energy constantly coursing through the universe. The earth's primary concern, of course, is with the sun and its relentless stream of life-giving (and life-destroying) radiation. As you know, the ozone layer acts as a filter for the more harmful rays, allowing only those frequencies conducive to life to strike the surface.

Just as the human body's immune system has defenses against invading agents, so does the earth take action to protect itself from damaging cosmic events. The use of cloud covers, storms, wind to cool or heat, and alterations in the chemical composition of the oceans, all serve to mitigate the effect of potentially damaging radiation. A thunderstorm, with its brilliant forks of lightning slicing the sky, results not only from energy built up on the earth's surface, but also to release harmful levels of energy erupting from the sun's surface. The energy is finely focused into lightning rather than being allowed to disperse more generally and with greater harm.

As mentioned before, all levels of organism structure communicate with and affect each other. A severe disturbance in one level will ripple through adjacent levels, manifesting obliquely, almost symbolically. As the health of an organism depends on the health of its constituent parts, a larger organism must be made aware if its smaller organismic elements are in distress. For example, a person with cancer will not feel a tumor growing inside him at first, but may feel other symptoms which ultimately cause sufficient concern to bring to a physician's notice, where the correct diagnosis can be made. A disease state does not announce itself in complete fidelity to the larger organism of which it is a part, but sufficient distress will bring awareness and attempts at corrective healing.

AIDS : Symbol of Global Health Breakdown

AIDS is not primarily a human disease, nor the result of a mysterious virus appearing from nowhere a decade or so ago. AIDS, rather, is a "stepped down" version of the breakdown of the global immune system. It is a reflection of the earth's condition as it struggles to maintain its health against the electromagnetic onslaught wreaked by the human species.

You may have noticed the changes in weather patterns over the last decade. Each winter seems to be the coldest on record, while summers are unusually torrid. Drought affects large areas of the Midwest and West Coast, while other areas of the country are lashed by severe storms and unprecedented snowfall. It seems as if the normal boundaries of weather behavior are being broken and unusually destructive patterns emerge.

This is the natural result of the earth's struggle to maintain its health while the human species cripples its immune system, its protective electromagnetic shield and sensor. No longer can the earth anticipate changes in solar radiation in time to properly alter the atmosphere and minimize damage to the surface. No longer has the earth the full use of its atmospheric resources to regulate weather patterns. Instead, its highly precise control is lost as it struggles merely to retain some awareness of cosmic conditions and to take protective action. Its regulatory actions are no longer smooth, precise, and perfectly balanced, but crude and volatile. The result is the deterioration of weather patterns as experienced over the last decade.

Not coincidentally, the last decade also saw the first case of AIDS, with the number of infected now in the millions. Because the human organism—at the species level—communes with and is affected by the larger global organism, it replicates the earth's struggle with its own version of immune system breakdown. While attributing the disease to a virus, a tiny agent invading the body, the disease truly arises from a larger context, from the earth's impaired condition. The relationship between the AIDS virus and the human body precisely reflects that between the human species and the earth: a deliberate, though unconscious, destruction of the immune system leading to systemic breakdown.

The human species, in its exuberant love of technology and scientific progress, electrified the earth before it had any knowledge of the potential effects. Unlike some human acts, taken with conscious knowledge of the destruction they would cause and undertaken anyway, the stringing of electrical wires across the globe had no known ill effects to the human species or any other. There was no deliberate attempt to harm the earth, no information that such might result, because human knowledge of the earth's electromagnetic field was—and is—primitive if not nonexistent.

The AIDS virus conducts itself exactly the same way within the human body. It does not act with the deliberate intent to cause harm or to destroy its host; it simply uses the host's body to replicate itself. In the process, however, it damages the immune system to the point where the body can no longer fight off infection and invading foreign agents; thus the body is laid bare to be ravaged by a host of diseases and infections.

Because the AIDS virus does not work in harmony with its host's body, but unconsciously destroys it, its activities are ultimately suicidal: the host's body dies and so must the virus. Extrapolate this process to the higher level of organismic structure, the earth as acted upon by the human species, and draw your own conclusions.

Treatment of AIDS from an Energetic Perspective

The current approach to treatment of AIDS is the latest extension of orthodox medicine's traditional view of the body and disease: there must be an isolated agent causing the illness which can be destroyed by drugs or radiation and stymied by a vaccine. Little attention is paid to the social and environmental contexts of which the person is a part, much less the global organism and its effect on the human organism. As a result, current approaches to treatment of AIDS are misguided, harmful, and ultimately ineffective.

True healing of AIDS—as well as cancer, heart disease, and other degenerative diseases resulting from technology's assault on the human and global bodies—can only come about when much more is understood about the electromagnetic basis of life. As medicine now stands, the body is seen primarily in chemical and biological terms; electromagnetism is peripheral at best. Recent findings relating to the harmful effects of certain bands and strengths of electromagnetic radiation—sitting before a computer, a television, X-rays, nuclear radiation—are the first pieces of the larger puzzle which must be assembled before a genuine understanding of human and global health can emerge. As long as treatment of AIDS remains rooted in the orthodox perspective, it is doomed to temporary patch-ups like using AZT, itself a drug carrying powerfully damaging effects, rather than effecting genuine healing.

The danger is that, as the earth's condition is reflected in the human condition, if the earth is allowed to deteriorate further AIDS will be only one health problem among many, and an increasingly minor one. As things stand now, you are fortunate in that AIDS can be transmitted only through intimate, not casual, contact. There are latent potentials for diseases carrying AIDS' lethal effects, transmitted far more casually than AIDS.

True healing of AIDS, then, must begin with healing the human species' effects on the planet and on an understanding of the dangers of electromagnetic radiation unleashed upon it. While this seems a monumental undertaking, and of little comfort to those presently afflicted, ultimately it is the only lasting "cure" for AIDS, and for those more deadly and easily transmissible diseases of which it is the portent.

As a temporary measure for those presently afflicted, it should be obvious that the worst possible setting in which to expect mitigation of symptoms is a hospital room. Hospitals are shrines of modern technology, built upon concrete slabs sealing off the earth's healing energies and allowing no beneficial solar and cosmic rays to bathe their patients. The best setting for those suffering from diseases caused by electromagnetic disturbance—principally cancer and AIDS—is, obviously, a natural setting far from concrete, electricity, and telephone. Sites near water are best, as water interacts with solar and lunar forces in a lively, energetic fashion, creating fields of exuberant healing.

The point is to find locales with their electromagnetic fields relatively undisturbed, so the crippled human energy field can be realigned by the natural energies of earth, moon, and sun. Food untainted by chemical fertilizer or pesticide, grown in areas of bucolic tranquility, is literally more nutritious than food grown by traditional chemical farms, and further carries an energy pattern in greater harmony with the human body.

The Larger Meaning of AIDS

Much more is involved in the creation of AIDS than its miniature reflection of the human species' attack on the global immune system. Every disease is a symbol, and in its putative "cause" and especially in its symptoms, carries a host of clues as to the underlying reasons for its manifestation. Because AIDS is a highly social disease—in its mode of transmission and in its effect on society as a whole as you grapple with the medical, economic, religious, and social implications— its origin may be understood as an expression of deep-seated issues long simmering beneath surface awareness, now boiling to the surface of consciousness.

Issues of sexuality, particularly homosexuality, are forced into the open in a culture long suffering from puritanical repression and homophobia. Compassion toward the oppressed, downtrodden, and forgotten rises to the fore as the afflicted groups read like a comprehensive list of society's most maligned clusters: gays, drug addicts, minorities, prostitutes. Society is forced to face the depths and limits of its compassion for those afflicted, who carry no badges of socially approved honor to "earn" their compassion, instead forcing the question of human life's intrinsic worth, stripped of honorable ornamentation.

AIDS forces closer scrutiny of the medical establishment, built as it is on the mechanistic view of the body as a machine prone to invasion by foreign agents, to be treated with new parts, drugs, and surgery. The AIDS virus is perversely immune to medicine's attempts to pin it down on a microscopic glass and reveal its secrets. It mutates at a maddening rate.

Given medicine's failure to understand the virus or devise vaccines and cures, the previously secure foundation on which medicine placed itself, far above the scrutiny of mere mortals, is now shaken as clamors for faster results bring medicine's procedures and assumptions to light, as well as the grotesque profiteering of drug companies growing rich off the deathbed suffering of the afflicted. Those howling for faster results are themselves mired in western medicine's traditional worldview, of course, demanding drugs, shots, treatments; but the process is the first step toward shaking free medicine's iron-grip monopoly on medical treatment and defrocking its previously exalted high priests.

These are but a few of the larger ramifications and meanings of the AIDS epidemic. We have discussed others in greater detail in our first book. The point here is to illustrate that a "social event" like AIDS always carries deep hidden meanings, forcing society to challenge its cherished assumptions and institutions as they fail to adequately address a new challenge. We submit that no cure will be forthcoming—and, indeed, more devastating viral agents may be looming—unless the human species' attack on the earth's electromagnetic immune system is ended. For just as your body's cells must die when your body releases life, so must all species-organisms perish if the global organism's life is extinguished.

The Body Electromagnetic:
Good (And Bad) Vibrations

In the last chapter we discussed AIDS from an electromagnetic perspective rather than through western medicine's traditional biochemical approach. In this essay we delve more deeply into understanding the body as a fundamentally electromagnetic entity. Doing so allows not only for a better understanding of how the body works, but also makes clear the link between consciousness and physical form, a bond long broken from the perspective of dualistic, Cartesian science.

The Electromagnetic Universe

First we must define electromagnetism. Splitting the word into its two components, "electro" refers to the basic component of the physical system, a pulsating energetic field; "magnetic" refers to this energy's intrinsic property of attraction—and, by implication, nonattraction or resistance—which governs its activity. At its most basic level, then, the universe is composed of infinitesimally tiny units of energy whose dance of attraction and resistance creates and supports matter and its attendant physical laws.

These tiny units of energy constantly blink in and out of the physical system. Each unit's strength determines the type of structure of which it is a part: for instance, air, water, or solid. Each time the energy units blink "into" the universe their strength is determined by several factors: their intensity on the preceding blink, any variations in the surrounding energy field which affects them, and, most important, any "intent" carried in the consciousness of nearby entities.

All action originates as thought. Once a given course of action is decided upon, intent carries the action from thought to physical manifestation. Because the minute energy sparks weaving the physical world are themselves conscious, they are exquisitely sensitive to the intent of bodies of consciousness within their field of activity. They respond appropriately by altering the strength and position of their charge upon each successive "blink" into physical existence.

To take a prosaic example, imagine that you wish to pick up a pencil. That pencil, seemingly dead, immobile, and insensate, is in truth a swarming, pulsating field of vibration (as physicists will agree). The boundaries of the "pencil field" are cleanly demarcated; immediately surrounding it is "empty space," meaning the energy units there pulse so softly as to be beneath the threshold of your sensory perception.

To pick up the pencil, your intent to pick it up compels your hand to move toward it, meaning that with each successive blink the energy field creating your hand is experienced as moving toward the pencil. This activity sends ripples of consciousness to the energy field sustaining the pencil. Given that no physical laws are violated by the act, you experience picking up the pencil, meaning the "pencil field" submits to the strength of your intent and, with each successive blink, travels with identical speed and trajectory with your "hand field." Thus you experience picking up the pencil.

The key to the process is intent, intent born of consciousness. The physical system exists because the Source *intends* that it exist, and this relationship of intent-to-matter pervades all of creation. Consciousness precedes form and animates activity. Any intention to act sends ripples of consciousness to those within the local sphere of activity, whether animate or inanimate to your perception.

The Human Blueprint

Because energy is organized according to the intent of consciousness, all forms in the physical system have been designed to grant expression to a particular focus or slant of consciousness. That is, the Source splinters its consciousness into an infinitude of unique potentials, each of which finds expression through an appropriate physical form. The species on your planet did not evolve in a haphazard, random way, but are expressions of bodies of consciousness existing in eternal viability beyond the space-time limitations of physical life.

The human body's form, structure, and function thus carry a host of clues about the purpose of human life. The most obvious and significant feature of human form is that you walk upright. Rather than marking a break from four-footed ancestors, as evolutionary theory would propose, the human form was designed to hold its brain high above the earth and above its other organs.

The earth constantly emits a stream of electromagnetic energy which dissipates rapidly as it climbs toward the atmosphere. This earth energy bathes all creatures living on the surface. *As a general rule*, the closer an animal's brain is to the earth's surface, the more it will be governed by instinct rather than rational thought. That is, the earth's energy is strongest at the surface, binding surface-dwelling creatures to an earth-based, largely instinctual existence.

As the brain is lifted higher from the surface, as in mammals, the influence of cosmic forces increases as the earth's force diminishes. If earth energy is the deep, instinctual bond to animal nature, the cosmic forces, or "star energy," govern the higher faculties of reason, creativity, and spirituality.

Not only is the human brain held high above the earth, then, but also above the body's other organs. A species' design expresses the desired balance between instinct and reason. Most mammals, being four-legged, hold the brain at the same height above the earth as the other organs, particularly the genitals. As the site of reproduction is the strongest bond to instinctual behavior, an animal form carrying brain and genitals at the same height above the earth grants equal emphasis to instinct and reason. Such animals are capable of rational thought—weighing choices, making decisions—but such thought is largely colored by instinctual patterns and offers little room for creativity.

Because the human form carries the brain well above the genitals, the emphasis is focused on the fruits of rational and creative thought. Humanity's purpose in the overall scheme, its particular focus of consciousness, is rational thought. By holding its head "in the clouds," the human form is delivered from earth-based instinctual patterns and rides the cosmic forces to peaks of intellectual and creative thought.

A further feature of human form is its highly efficient design. Nature's most efficient shape is the axis, a slender tube, as in a tree or worm. The further a form deviates from the axis shape the less efficient it is, and the more energy is required to sustain it. Some animals must consume several times their body weight every day to sustain themselves; and large mammals graze constantly. The human form, whose healthy shape approximates an axis, is highly efficient and requires relatively little food energy to sustain it. Thus humanity is spared the continuous grazing and foraging of many species and is free to pursue its true purpose: the celebration and achievements of rational and creative thought.

The Body Electromagnetic

Physicists confirm that objects perceived by your senses as solid are, in truth, nothing more than waves and patterns of energy. Further, a small number of atoms are responsible for sustaining the fantastical variety of creation; as a few amino acids are the foundation of the body's inconceivably complex and diverse structures. What western science has been unable to determine is the cause of the body's differentiation as it progresses from a single cell to the adult form. Given that just a few amino acids are the building blocks of the body, and that the DNA is identical in every cell, what provides the blueprint for the body's form?

When the universe blinks "off" out of physical expression, it does not switch into a neutral state of nonexistence, but rather returns to a state of pure consciousness. You can imagine a duplicate universe, one containing all physically manifesting forms as ideas, pure consciousness, rather than as structures. It is this pool of consciousness that holds the blueprints for all physical forms. The body's growth from embryo to child to adulthood to death is regulated by the nonphysical blueprint for the body which blinks from pure consciousness into the physical system.

Upon blinking into the physical system, the intent to sustain the body's form is expressed as an electromagnetic pattern, a grid of intent. The elements you know as atoms are magnetically attracted into this pattern, there to hold their place in the overall structure; countless such atoms coagulate into molecules, and then into ever larger structures of greater complexity. The body's form is not determined by the DNA alone, but principally by the unseen blueprint which pulses into physical expression as an electromagnetic grid of intent.

The key to the formation of the body's various organs and tissues thus lies not in the DNA or any biochemical process, but in vibration. The electromagnetic patterns for the various organs differ in frequency, attracting atomic elements in various proportions and patterns. If you could hear them, each organ would sing a different tone; if you could see them, each would glow a different color.

The body, then, is a complex organization of electromagnetic frequencies creating a pattern of vibration. All of the other systems of the body's functioning—biological, chemical, neurological—ride atop and reflect the vibrational pattern which is the body's source.

Electromagnetic Effects on the Body

Since the body is essentially electromagnetic energy, and since all elements of the physical system are electromagnetic as well, the picture of a universe of discrete objects separated by empty space begins to break down. In its place grows the awareness of physical forms composed of and swimming in electromagnetic energy, these forms interacting constantly through the dance of attraction and resistance.

The human body regularly emits and absorbs electromagnetic radiation. Concern is now growing that some electromagnetic radiation may have deleterious effects on the body's health. With the understanding outlined above, we can see that radiation which simply carries information to the body is salubrious, while radiation so intense as to interfere with the body's functioning is harmful.

Radiation is harmful when it is of an intensity or frequency that interferes with the body's natural vibrational state. The human body is tuned to vibrate faster than the earth's pulsation and much slower than the sun's fierce cacophony, allowing you to "stand between" earth and sun. In a natural setting, the body absorbs telluric and cosmic radiation in the proper proportion to maintain optimum health. Any interference pattern which disrupts this natural balance prevents the body's elements from communicating with each other and prevents the body's electromagnetic pattern from pulsating in full strength into physical being. The result can be a breakdown in health, physical, emotional, or mental.

By electromagnetic interference we mean a far broader range of influence than high-voltage power lines and microwave ovens. Since all physical form is essentially electromagnetic, a toxic chemical, a nutritional imbalance, or cigarette smoke are all essentially electromagnetic influences in that they interfere with the body's electromagnetic pattern. The invisible transmission of energy from electrical devices is just now beginning to be recognized as carrying potential deleterious effects, but at base it carries the same influence as the more obvious, physically observable sources: interference with the body's electromagnetic pattern.

The explosion of cancers in this century is the direct result of the toxic soup in which you now live, where air, water, food, and even the airwaves are contaminated. Consider for a moment what cancer is: an explosive growth of cells which interferes with the body's healthy functioning. Such a growth often occurs when an external influence on the body creates an interference pattern, meaning the body's electromagnetic blueprint is not expressed in full vitality; the transmission is garbled.

When you walk past a television set, your body's field interferes with the set's reception, scrambling the picture. When a toxic chemical or powerful radiation impacts the human body, it scrambles the reception and expression of the information pulsing from the realm of consciousness. It prevents the pattern from expressing. The atomic structures which previously received instruction as to their arrangement are deprived of their directions and lose their cohesive identity with the larger body. As a result, they reproduce without restraint. Receiving scrambled instructions, or no instructions at all, they are cut loose from the tight, efficient pattern organizing the body.

The same occurs at death. Once consciousness departs the body and the organizational blueprint no longer blinks into the physical system, the elements comprising the body lose their instructions locking them into place and imposing cohesion and unity. Like schoolchildren unleashed for recess, order is lost as each element is freed to pursue its private fulfillment and decay sets in.

Begin to perceive yourself as a field of pulsating vibration, both sending radiation to and receiving information from other objects and the seemingly empty space between them. Knowing that you are far closer to the vibration of the earth than the sun, be aware of what vibration you allow into your field. Consider that devices simulating the sun's qualities—heat, intense vibration, high frequency—may have deleterious effects on your body's earth-based vibrational pattern.

Perceive food and drink as electromagnetic substances, and consider how and where they are grown or produced, with what possible chemical contamination, and how they are processed. The less time between a food's harvesting and your ingestion of it, and the less profit-seeking intent motivating its processing, the more nutritious it will be.

Finally, see other people as more than flesh and blood, but as electromagnetic forms as well. The human form is designed to exchange information with other bodies from about six feet apart, with the fidelity of transmission increasing as bodies near. You hug those you love because your bodies urge you to exchange the information they carry, one to the other, mirroring your verbal exchange. Those you have not seen for a long time, you hug more tightly because more information must be exchanged. Sex compels you because an energetic, passionate encounter releases torrents of information and healing. Children need constant affection because they unconsciously absorb the beliefs and principles of their culture through contact with adults. Western culture's traditional discouragement of touch and affection is in no small measure responsible for the culture's current sickness, for an essential means of communication and healing has been blocked.

In the decades ahead, the understanding that you are swimming in a sea of electromagnetic energy, which weaves the pattern for your body and all other physical forms as well, will become common knowledge. Those who incorporate this understanding into their consciousness now can both avoid deleterious effects on their health and mental well-being and affirmatively fashion an environment with their bodies' health and harmony held paramount.

❖   ❖   ❖

As a supplement to Alexander's discussion of the importance of physical contact in maintaining physical and mental health, the following is an excerpt from a private session in which Alexander addresses a young man's reluctance to relinquish his freedom and independence for commitment to a woman; the young man felt he incorporated many feminine qualities in his psyche and was therefore "balanced" without needing a partner.

The issue really isn't one of internal balance between male and female elements, as this is the ideal in every person, with either male or female traits given emphasis depending on the chosen sex. Every healthy individual should maintain such a balance. The issue, rather, is instead how a life partner helps maintain psychic, emotional, and physical balance.

The body is basically electromagnetic energy. Each "particle" of the body is charged not only with energy but with *information*. This information, about the body's condition, one's emotional state, a memory store of recent events, and the surrounding environment, is transmitted from "cell" to "cell" in the energy field surrounding the body. Its primary purpose is to keep all elements of the body apprised of all other elements; this communication between the body's energy cells is how the liver knows what the toes are doing, should that information be vitally necessary.

The secondary purpose of this information is to apprise others of your mental, physical, emotional, and spiritual condition. Any time you come in contact with another, information is exchanged on levels hidden from sensory awareness. One of the great benefits of a life partner is that regular close contact ensures that another body, another body of information and energy, is regularly apprised of your condition. This has consequences and ramifications you cannot imagine. In many cases, incipient illnesses can be healed by another's energy field, especially when that person's thoughts of you are loving. An imbalance can be restored, a deficiency in the body's nutritional balance can be righted, an emotional ache soothed, and so on.

This is the reason why married people live longer than singles: a life partner literally heals the body. Rather than the body having to always heal itself of injuries to body or psyche, the task can be relinquished to another whose energy field is not disrupted at that time. So the "balance" referred to is not so much a balance of male-female energies but a far broader, all-encompassing balance of every aspect of the human condition: spiritual, emotional, mental, physical.

Now, a close and loving friend could provide most of this balancing, but presumably would not be having sex with you, and here is perhaps the strongest argument for a life partner who is also a lover. Naturally, the sex act brings you face to face in a heated, emotional, excited, passionate encounter. This facilitates the exchange of information across the chest and abdomen area. The compulsion many feel for sex, particularly men in your culture, reflects their desperate need for balancing, for sharing their thoughts and troubles with another, which in your culture a man is not permitted to openly express. He is therefore forced to express it nonverbally, through the sex act; this compulsion is misinterpreted as an urge for orgasm. Primarily, it is an urge to share oneself with another, and this unburdening and sharing is blocked in all ways but through sex.

Another reason for finding this solace in a lover or life-time companion rather than a friend is that by contractual or unspoken agreement, there is a commitment to each other, a loving bond of exclusivity binding the relationship. This communicates to the other that he or she is "special," opening the way for an even deeper and more complete exchange of information. Over time, the psyches intertwine and create a third entity, a hybrid energy form, which is replenished and added to whenever the couple is in close proximity.

So there are good reasons, good physical, emotional, mental, spiritual reasons for seeking companionship, a life-time companion, a lover, wife, husband. It is not merely social convention. The social convention derives from the uncon-scious recognition of the healing, balancing effects of routine contact with another.

You see why this should also hold true for homosexuals. The "balancing" is not so much of the male-female dichot-omy, but of a broader, gender-neutral nature. Among hetero-sexuals, there is the additional element of a male routinely being bathed by feminine energy, which does help balance him; the reverse is also true for women. But this in no way detracts from homosexuality as being as "normal" an expres-sion of human sexuality as heterosexuality.

Finally, Alexander's response to a reader's frustration over caring for an aging mother rounds out this chapter's discussion of the body electromagnetic:

"I have a mother who is 90 years old. She is slowly losing touch with the appropriateness of things, is incontinent, re-fuses to wear decent clothes, is hard of hearing and refuses to

wearing a hearing aid. As a result I am exhausted, sad, angry, impatient, etc. Why are people living so long when they are such a great burden?"

Building on our essay about the electromagnetic construction of the body and the consciousness and intent which sustain it, helps us to address the disturbing increase in Alzheimer's disease and those experiencing progressive mental and physical decay as they age.

The normal cycle of life allows for constructive activity and purposeful living at every stage. Old age is meant to be a gradual release of middle age's intense focus on the mechanics of physical existence—children, career, finances—and mirrors childhood in keeping one foot in physical existence while dabbling the other in the spiritual realm.

As one comes to understand that intent and consciousness animate physical form, one appreciates the power of belief in creating one's reality. Beliefs are the foundation of all mental activity, filtering the flow of daily events, coloring one's perception and action. Beliefs provide the background field of mental activity upon which all other thought and activity are based. As a result, beliefs carry great power to influence the health of the body and mind.

If one believes that aging necessarily means physical decay, this belief will literally restrict the body's pulsation from nonphysical blueprint to physical expression, compromising the body's full vitality. Over time, as the flow from consciousness to form is increasingly impeded, not only physical decay results, but mental decline as well. The body and mind are literally starved for their full quotient of sustaining energy.

The increase of Alzheimer's and similar conditions reflects your culture's beliefs about life, aging, and death. If the purpose of life is reduced to material considerations, as it is for most, then those who no longer produce for the economy are seen as having no value to society. If aging is seen as decay, and death as an end rather than a portal to new adventure, the body will faithfully reflect this belief through degeneration.

Quite apart from this process is the soul's determination of when physical life should be released. Death is always chosen, but not necessarily when it is convenient for others. The soul's purpose is paramount. Even if severely restricted by the collapse of physical and mental structures, a soul will attempt to fulfill its life purpose, however attenuated its power to do so. Only when a soul's life task has been fulfilled, or it is evident that no further gains can be made through a given physical vehicle, will the soul release its grip on life and cease the pulsation into physical form.

Gardening With Spirit:
The Conscious Gardener

All earthly life is consciousness housed in form. That is, the consciousness animating a life form is its true self, its core of being, and the form it assumes grants physical expression to the intent and purpose of that consciousness. Consciousness precedes form.

All life forms sharing your planet are subsumed under the rubric of "earth consciousness." This earth consciousness divides and splinters into a multitude of form, the better to grant variety, diversity, and thus stability to the natural order. Perhaps the most significant division from your standpoint is that between the animal and vegetable kingdoms.

The fundamental distinction between plant and animal kingdoms is that animals explore the use of rational thought, in various strengths and focuses, while vegetation's purpose is to live on a pure level of undiluted harmony with the natural order. Rational thought, the hallmark of the animal kingdom, means taking a step away from absolute trust and harmony with the earth. Most animals, for example, must make some effort to find their food; they cannot stand in one place all their lives and expect their food to come to them. Plants, by contrast, are literally rooted to the earth in the same spot from birth to death; the choice to experience life in such a form must carry a deep, abiding faith in the earth's beneficence in providing the nutrients, water, and sunlight necessary to sustain life, all without moving an inch.

With the freedom and mobility of the animals' focus on rational thought comes a certain loss of connection with the earth, a loss of faith in the natural order. Many animals spend much of their lives in the eternal dance of predator and prey, and for them life is rich with danger, skill and cunning. This is the choice, this is the division: between total rootedness to the earth and trust in its providence; or a rational focus, coupled with mobility, which separates animals from the earth.

The Vegetable Kingdom

At a high, amorphous level of consciousness, all vegetation is joined in a common body of consciousness. As you experience the world of vegetation, however, you behold a richly diverse family of innumerable species, some staking claim to but a few acres of land and found nowhere else. Because each physical form has behind it a distinct consciousness, you can appreciate how the overarching "vegetation consciousness" splinters and divides into increasingly fine focuses of intent, animating the profusion of plant forms.

Each species of plant thus expresses a particular aspect of planthood. Some opt for quiescent indolence, like grasses beside a meandering river. Some go for drama: bursting forth from the soil in the spring, shooting brilliant blossoms toward the sun, then dying with their glory still fresh. Some are tenacious and methodical, like vines slowly covering a brick wall year after year. Some choose to mirror the seasons, like deciduous trees blossoming in the spring, flourishing into summer's verdant display, then bursting into autumn flame before winter's long dormancy. Others, the conifers, wear the same green mantle throughout the cycle of seasons.

While all plants have methods of propagating themselves, spreading their seeds to advantage in the hopes of perpetuating themselves, of particular interest to this discussion are those plants whose method of seed propagation—encasing them in nutrient-rich bodies—is so beneficial, indeed essential, to the animal kingdom.

Fruits, Vegetables, and Man

The earth system was set up on a system of mutually beneficial relationships among species, between animal and vegetable kingdoms, and so on. One such relationship is between animals and fruits and vegetables. Animals benefit from the nutrients held in fruits and vegetables, while plants benefit from the seed-scattering activities of animals; a seed can pass through an animal's digestive tract and emerge intact and unharmed many miles from its parent plant. Thus a symbiotic relationship is inherently built into the association between mobile animals and stationary fruiting plants.

Rather than simply foraging and eating whatever wild foods were available, early man began to systematically raise crops as food. This not only ensured a more consistent food supply, but also allowed the transition from nomadic hunter-gatherers to stable communities, the precursor of the modern city and town.

Wild vegetation flourishes without any help from man, but what we might call "tamed" vegetation—cultured food plants—gradually intertwined its fate and consciousness with man's. An openly symbiotic relationship has been established (as opposed to the unconscious symbiotic relationship between wild vegetation and other animals) in which food crops have come to depend on man to provide necessary growing conditions, and the plants are assured of propagation because their seeds are gathered for planting the following year.

Because man's primary focus is rational thought and physical manipulation, it follows that millennia of selective breeding have created plant species bearing little likeness to their wild ancestors, and which could now survive but poorly without man's care. The toughness has been bred out of many species as farmers prized tender, delicious produce; the plants have lost their wild adaptability in favor of man's nurturance. Just as domesticated cats and dogs may be born with their canine and feline instincts intact but attenuated, willingly joining with man as his companion animals in exchange for food and shelter, so too do domesticated food plants now intertwine their consciousness with man's. A mutually dependent relationship has been forged and neither can survive without the other.

Plant Communication: Understanding Thought-Forms

Because domesticated food plants have so intertwined their consciousness with that of man and are dependent on human care to survive and flourish, it stands to reason that making contact with the consciousness of garden plants should be easier than communing with plants in wild places, indifferent as they are to man's presence. Now, the thought of contacting *any* plant's consciousness—wild or garden—may well raise a skeptical eyebrow among our readers. This underscores the great schism in western culture between man and the natural world. The notion that only human beings possess consciousness and souls is unique to your culture, and would be found laughable in any native culture. The relationship between man and plants is understood as a palpable, breathing, organic partnership by most native tribes.

Garden plants have so long been bred and nurtured by man that they are exquisitely attuned to human consciousness. They feel your moods when you hover near them; they know your attitudes and desires toward them; they are strengthened by thoughtful, tender care from a loving gardener's hand. Plants don't deal with symbols, as you communicate with others, but exchange thought-forms directly, without impediment. They sense and feel and know without distortion and are immune to the disingenuous masks and role playing you engage in with others of your species. Plants are always honest.

You know of "green thumbs" and "brown thumbs," those who can make everything grow and those who kill everything they touch. The difference lies not in the technical aspects of plant care, but in the soul of the gardener, its purity, harmony, and contentment, and in the attitude toward the plants being tended. Are they "objects" to be managed like green furniture, or are they accorded the respect due all living beings?

Many cultures have spawned mythologies of elves, fairies, gnomes, little people, devas, and so on, who live in the forest or the garden. These are anthropomorphic projections, of course, transforming the sensed bodies of consciousness into recognizable form. If yours is the age when mythologies are released in order to directly behold the truths behind them, how can you release the fairy-tale approach to plants and make direct contact with them? Knowing that garden plants are attuned to your consciousness and are eager to work in partnership with you, how can you openly acknowledge and communicate with your plants?

Briefly, let us discuss how communication on the level of pure thought-form takes place. Because you communicate through symbols, and symbols can be reproduced and sent anywhere around the globe, you need give no thought to limitations on your power to communicate; telephone wires, fax machines, and videotape will carry your messages everywhere. This is not the case with those beings who communicate through thought-forms. This pure, direct contact is at the level of consciousness, not physical symbol, and such communication depends on physical proximity to ensure the highest fidelity of transmission. The waves of energy swirling about the body dissipate rapidly with distance, so the closer two bodies stand, the purer the transmission of energy between them.

For effective man-plant communication to occur, you must release the natural human tendency to reduce your thoughts to speech and to speak them aloud, considering that to be effective communication. Plants don't have ears. They can't hear you. What you say falls away as into a black void, unheard and unheeded. If communication is to be effective, it must be offered so plants can receive the message, meaning it must be on the level of pure thought-form.

As a human adult, you have spent so many years thinking with language that you may have lost the understanding that thoughts precede language, even when tossing ideas about in your mind. A pure thought-form exists first as a grid of consciousness, only later "stepped down" to the level of symbolic speech, words and phrases through which you organize your thoughts and communicate them to others. Babies have thoughts but no speech; animals have thoughts but no speech. You operate on a "thought first-speech later" basis, but the time gap is so negligible that you may believe you think with words. You do not. Like babies, animals, and plants, your thoughts exist as pure consciousness first and foremost.

The primary rule of communicating with plants, therefore, is that you must release your emphasis on spoken language and return to the pure thought of infancy. At this level, thought-forms are organized not in a rational, logical sequence, but as emotional intensities. The greater the emotion wedded to a thought, the stronger its impact on oneself and those in proximity.

Weaving together the two key elements of physical proximity and communicating through thought-forms, we can offer a guide to communing with your plant friends. First, bring your hands around the plant, hovering within an inch of the plant's leaves. Plants do not appreciate being manhandled, excessively fondled or otherwise abused. Besides the obvious risk of physical injury, to touch a plant leaves a human residue which interferes with the plant's ability to release chemical messengers into the air. So it is best to bring your hands as close as possible but make no contact.

Second, in order to release the doggedly rational focus which is your gift and bane, close your eyes, take a few deep breaths, and try to simply be with the plant for a few moments. Don't ask it questions and don't offer advice. Simply be with the plant. Allow your energies to commingle at the nexus of your hands and its leaves. Know that voluminous quantities of information are being exchanged as your energetic bodies mingle, a process beyond rational comprehension.

Next you might make an offering of gratitude or love or appreciation to the plant, an amorphous burst of good will, not yet carrying specific information or request. Try to feel this offering building in your chest, then release it through your arms and feel it tingle at your fingertips, bathing the plant with pure energy. Allow a few moments for this to sink in; it helps assure the plant that your intent is benign and respectful. Again, as a thought-form's strength is determined by the emotional charge behind it, try to boost your feelings of good will to their highest emotional pitch.

Once these initial greetings and gifts have been exchanged—as is custom in human culture too—you may proceed to business. If the plant is doing well, you may simply want to express your thankfulness for the nourishment it will offer your body. If a flower, you may appreciate its beauty. If a houseplant, cherish its air-purifying skills and the verdant cheer it brings you.

If a plant seems unhappy, is failing to thrive, you may then move to specifics: communicating your concern and asking what the plant needs. Again, focus on pure thought-forms rather than speech. Rather than ask, "Is it the mumps?", create a receptive space in your mind, a space to be filled only by the plant. You may visualize this, if you wish, as an area of your mind standing empty for the exclusive use of your plants to communicate their needs. This is a stretch for most people, but it has a literal validity in that you are creating a psychic vacuum and, as nature abhors vacuums, *something* must fill it. By affirming that only your plants can fill it with their needs, you literally carve a space in the psyche for the exclusive use of your plants.

Now, remember, your plants will not verbalize their needs. They will not recite a litany of aches and pains; and, in all likelihood, you will not immediately receive their messages. As trained as you are to focus on symbolic means of communication, it takes time for a thought-form to burrow into your psyche and gradually work its way into conscious awareness. The process can take hours or days. Leave it alone, don't bother it by thinking about it.

At first, nothing at all may surface and you may find yourself silently agreeing with those who mock "the weirdo talking to plants." Several highly unusual processes are at work: first, your attempts to deliberately communicate with plants, which your western psyche is inexperienced at doing; second, your plants' inexperience at communicating directly with humans; and third, your psyche's processing of direct thought-forms from plant sources. Enough to keep the healthiest of psyches in turmoil at first! So the process will not bear fruit overnight.

There are also vast differences among people as to their degree of sensitivity, limits on conscious awareness of the process. While some can sit yards away from the garden and receive volumes of detailed instructions, most will share less dramatic communication. Among those whose psyches are in the "normal" range, messages from plants will most likely manifest as sudden hunches, urges, feelings.

You may be shopping in a nursery and feel a sudden urge to buy a particular fertilizer. You may find yourself consumed with thoughts of water, a signal from a thirsty plant. You may feel an urge to lie in the sun and soak up its rays, possibly a sign from a plant suffering in the shade. The trick will be discerning between your own thoughts and desires, and recognizing messages from your plants. As a rule, a message from a plant will gradually grow in intensity and be impervious to "reasoning" it away. If you tell yourself that you don't want to get skin cancer by lying in the sun, this rational thought will not diminish the urge to soak up the sun's rays—which you may ultimately divine as being the plant's call of distress. You can then take remedial action.

The Overlighting Devas

A step beyond communicating with individual plants as outlined above is making contact with the "devas," those bodies of consciousness hovering over a garden, not attached to any specific plant. An analogy would be your relationship to your higher self, with its knowledge of all your probable and reincarnational selves. If you grow tomatoes, for example, then in addition to the consciousness of each individual plant, a "tomato deva," or overlighting tomato consciousness, will permeate the garden. To make contact with such devas is more difficult than with single plants because no physical contact is possible, no direct exchange of energies. Instead, communication must take place solely as the exchange of pure thought-forms.

For those confident about their abilities, the best way to contact these devas is by sitting fairly close to the garden, no more than ten yards away. Close your eyes, take a few deep breaths, and try to create a pure meditative state. Then announce that you are receptive to communication from the devas and would like to join in partnership with them for the benefit of all.

You will know when a deva communicates: there will be no mushy greetings, no mention of "love and light," no squishy sentiment. Instead, there will be a series of direct commands, clear and precise, as to what the garden needs. Devas are all business, often brusque. They do not so much engage in dialogue as issue commands. Having a notebook and pen handy is a good idea, to catch the stream of instructions.

If this strikes you as harsh and unfriendly, such is your interpretation, not the devas' intent. They are not human and do not share your consciousness, your gregarious, social sensibilities. It is not their nature to exchange pleasantries to grease the wheels of polite conversation; they have no such conventions. Plants communicate through direct thought-forms, and the bursts of information you receive are responses to your stated desire to help your plants flourish. For warm-blooded affection and loyalty, turn to your dog or cat.

"Getting in touch with nature" can be more than an over-used phrase. As in any field, repetition, persistence and desire affect ultimate success. How much effort and time you put into conscious gardening determines the depth and endurance of the bond you create, your ability to discern your plants' messages. The payoff is a luxuriously healthy garden offering a bounty of highly nutritious food to sustain you in good health another year, so that you may work with your garden's heirs in the seasons to come.

Just Say Yes:
Drugs and Human Consciousness

As the "war against drugs" is used as the pretext for governmental restrictions on personal freedom, and as the "war" strains society's law enforcement, educational, and family structures beyond the breaking point, it behooves the thinking person to look past the slogans and simplistic thinking to find a deeper understanding of the "crisis" and how it came to be.

The Nature of Human Consciousness

First, let us look at human consciousness and why and how it is affected by the ingestion of mind-altering substances. Two main influences affect the activity of the human psyche: innate, built-in restrictions on the content of conscious mental activity; and societal mores, values, and beliefs which further restrict the range of "acceptable" thought patterns.

When you consider all the information existing in the realm of pure consciousness—where the entire historical sweep exists as a swirl of eternally viable probabilities and linear time does not exist—you recognize how limited is your everyday waking awareness. Your mind stands as the portal between your psyche and the world around you, feeding your store of daily experience up to the psyche and, in turn, granting physical expression to urges pulsating from the psyche. Your mind is "tethered" to the track of linear time, following its drip-by-drip flow of moments, shutting out awareness of events and processes occurring in the nonphysical realms of pure consciousness.

In addition, your society further restricts the free flow of such information due to its emphasis on the material world as the only valid reality. Almost everyone has had premonitions, hunches, flashes of intuition, prescient dreams, and so on. Yet because society cannot reduce these events to atoms and dissect them under the microscope, they are dismissed as coincidence or hoax. So the vast realm of consciousness, which offers so much wisdom and guidance to cultures open to its influence, is locked outside the gate of western culture, scorned and repudiated.

Human consciousness is one tiny strand of the Consciousness from which it flows, restricted to experiencing life on one planet through symbolic manipulation, human community, and spiritual search. In addition, each human culture wears culturally imposed blinders which further restrict the range of acceptable thought and behavior. This is the setup of human life into which each person is born.

The Vegetable Kingdom:
Kinship with Humanity

Let us state without elaboration that the world of plants is as bristling with intelligence and consciousness as any mobile species. You can think of the globe as having two surfaces: water, under which teem myriad species of animate life and vegetation; and land, upon which grows a carpet of intelligence, the plant world.

It can be no coincidence that the plant world provides all the necessities for human life—food, clothing, shelter, medicine, dyes, ornaments. While the plant world exists for its own purpose and can thrive in the absence of human company, support of human and other mammalian species is a "plus" for the plant world, an enriching element of their experience. When you ingest a plant, for however brief a time that plant's consciousness commingles with yours, offering the plant a unique experience of transspecies consciousness. You have the same experience as well, of course, but your mind is far less attuned to consciously experiencing the blend of human/plant consciousness.

So the human-plant relationship is symbiotic, with plants providing the essentials of human existence while man, through agriculture, landscaping, and ingestion of plants, offers the plant world enriched experience.

Mind-Altering Plants:
The Original Teachers

Among the uncountable species of plants offering life and comfort to humanity, a relative few contain compounds which directly alter human consciousness. To understand the process, let us look briefly at the relationship between consciousness and the body.

The body is built to reinforce the restricted scope of human consciousness. That is, its chemical processes form an elaborate framework funneling the swarms of consciousness which bathe you, unseen, into narrow bands of vibration granted access to the brain: these are your senses. Visible light and audible sound are simply two slivers of vibration which paint symbolic pictures of color and sound through which you perceive dense objects and their movement. Taste and smell are your narrow perception of life energies emanating from living beings. Touch is your navigational aid, keeping you from harm and steering you toward pleasure. All five senses have as their primary purpose helping you to navigate a clear course through the material world; secondarily, they reinforce the inborn and culturally imposed limits on human consciousness by not permitting most of the swirling energy fields about you to reach conscious awareness.

There are dangers in structuring human consciousness this way: danger that the ego, the identification with one body and fear for its survival, will rise to supremacy; danger that the twin pillars of human life, spirit and reason, will be forgotten in favor of gross materialism; danger that the ability to love and feel fully will be crippled by unnatural cultural constraints on emotional expression; danger that the awareness of underlying unity and oneness with the cosmos will be lost.

To help protect humanity from expressing its potential for ego-based, materialistic, soulless culture—and the cultural chaos and disintegration inevitably following—among its store of helpful plants nature produces those containing compounds which alter human consciousness. In truth, they do not alter human consciousness as much as they restore it to a higher, truer, purer level of awareness, freed from a few of the inborn and cultural shackles narrowing experience. They untie the neurochemical straitjackets through which incoming energies are reduced to a few narrow bands of sensory impression; they release the dependence on symbolic experience of energy patterns, allowing a direct apprehension of realms of consciousness never experienced by everyday consciousness.

The brain, built to efficiently process incoming sensory data along rigidly wired neuronal pathways, is suddenly overwhelmed by floods of unfamiliar material, coupled with a breakdown of its ability to process this data along its normal channels. The result can be mental chaos: hallucinations and visions which, like dreams, the brain can only struggle to render in symbolic form. Given the dosage and nature of the chemical ingested, the brain may simply surrender its role as neuronal gatekeeper, allowing consciousness to soar freely without reducing experience to symbol or attempting a rational understanding of the experience.

Such a drug-induced shattering of normal consciousness contributes to the stability of the individual experiencing it and the larger culture to which he or she belongs. It does so because the latent dangers in the makeup of human consciousness are obviated:

1.   The danger that the ego, identifying itself as encased in a body demarcated by the skin, will rise to supremacy. By rising above the one-body/one-mind delusion of earthly experience into realms where one perceives that the physical body is simply a symbolic expression of a fraction of the greater psyche, one realizes that one's true self, one's eternally viable self, is unrelated to flesh; that flesh merely houses the spirit for a span of years and is then discarded.

2.   The danger that the symbiosis between material and spiritual focuses will be broken. As consciousness wedded to flesh, you are simultaneously spiritual and physical beings, using the physical body to navigate through the earthly medium while your higher purpose, your reason for being, flows from the nonphysical psyche.

In a healthy individual and culture, reason—manipulation of the physical world—and spirit—the nonphysical source and meaning of life—are joined, the twin tracks of human progress on which you ride. As western culture has long favored the material and retains an anachronistic, primitive spirituality, the happy union between spirit and reason is sundered, leaving you to thrash about without a spiritual compass.

A drug-induced experience can restore this symbiosis by plunging one headlong into realms of pure consciousness and spiritual awareness, righting the balance by total immersion into realms long forgotten, now restored. By literally experiencing the union of the spiritual with the physical body, one retains an indelible memory of the deep security and mastery one feels when gliding smoothly along the twin tracks of human existence.

3. The danger that one's emotional life will be crippled by unnatural cultural constraints. In your culture, which devalues the feminine and therefore most emotional expression, men particularly stagger through life with wounded psyches and bottled-up feelings which they dare not openly express. "Positive" emotions are permitted in some circumstances, but "negative" emotions—anger, hatred, jealousy—are "bad" and not to be given vent.

Some drugs are known to work directly on the emotional component of the psyche. MDMA, or Ecstasy, for example, is promoted as "opening the heart chakra" and allowing genuine emotional contact with others. In truth, Ecstasy works not by opening the heart chakra but by dissolving the armor encasing most western hearts. The experience is not a "supranormal" one, then—a flight through realms of the psyche—but is simply a restoration of the free-flowing emotions, deep bonding with others, and communion with nature one felt in early childhood. Hallucinogens also carry this heart opening as a side effect; as the ego's fierce protection of maintaining a socially acceptable facade dissolves, one's true inner life can emerge.

4. The danger that awareness of oneness with the cosmos will be lost. As western culture's basic theme is separation, it stands to reason that each individual is made to feel alone and vulnerable, either in a meaningless universe or before an omniscient and angry sky god. A virtually universal experience, whatever the drug, is the restoration of a feeling of oneness, the unity of all creation. While the direct experience of this oneness is lost as normal consciousness is restored, the memory can remain to inform one's actions and foster a sense of community with others and with nature.

There is almost a self-serving element in the plant world providing compounds which accelerate human consciousness and dissolve the dangerous delusions accompanying an excessively materialistic focus. For as is now playing out in your experience, a culture cut off from its spiritual source and thrilling to its technological prowess, unmediated by spiritual wisdom, ends up destroying the ecosystems which support it. In so doing, of course, countless species of plants are lost forever (in your probable reality).

As the rain forests are slashed and burned to the ground, innumerable plant species are lost. As you chop down forests to plant a few food crops, plant species are lost. As you pave over the earth, plant species are lost. All of western culture's destructive actions and thoughtless extermination of other species stem from an ego-based, materially focused consciousness devoid of genuine spiritual life. This is why the plant world offers, among its plenty, substances which check and balance against this dangerous potential of human consciousness.

Native Culture vs. Western Culture:
Sacrament or Recreation?

To this point it may seem we are glorifying drugs and offering no warnings about the dangers of misuse. In the material above, we offered an understanding of how these substances affect human consciousness and why they exist in nature. In a natural, wise, spiritually centered culture, such drugs are known as "plant teachers," treated with respect and never abused. You do not, however, live in such a culture, and so we must explore why drug use and abuse now grips western society.

In a native culture in which all the world swarms with life and consciousness, plants are known as living beings, some offering food, others offering medicine, others, the psychoactive plants, offering knowledge and wisdom. In western culture, where the natural world has been bled of spiritual life and all spiritual power centered in the hands of a sky god, the natural world is acknowledged to be living, yes, but certainly not endowed with consciousness, personality, or wisdom. Only humans have souls.

It naturally follows, then, that psychoactive substances are not treated with respect as plant teachers, to be used in a sacramental fashion in spiritual ceremonies. Instead, as the natural world is seen as a giant sandbox which one may rip apart with impunity, use of psychoactive plants is reduced to recreation, a good time, or a release from daily cares. "Getting high" becomes simply a way to pass the time, and drugs are not taken for the purpose of introspection, spiritual wisdom, or genuine connection with others.

Just as the body revels in a break from a sedentary lifestyle—a hike, a bike ride, a walk—so does human consciousness delight in occasionally stretching beyond its everyday limits. In a sacred, ritualistic context, this journey to other realms strengthens the user and his culture. In a culture harshly forbidding any such exploration, plant teachers are demoted to recreational agents used furtively and without the wise guidance of elders.

Whether used as sacrament or recreation, the allure of drugs is all the stronger in a culture based on egregious falsehoods leading to chaos and disintegration. Drugs offer temporary release from a chaotic and irrational world; a restoration, however slight, to the truer, richer experience available in realms of pure consciousness. The massive drug taking of the younger generation in the Sixties served as an escape valve releasing the unbearable pressures building in a culture founded on monumental falsehoods.

Today the big worry is that young people will be ruined by drugs; yet adolescence is the stage of life when the psyche is wide open to as rich and varied a store of experience as it can absorb, so the attraction to drugs, to mystical experience and altered perception, is never greater. And every questioning youth, staring at the smoldering wreckage of the earth his elders have left him, naturally senses the spiritual destitution which has so cheapened his inheritance, and seeks new ways of being and thinking lest his generation be the last.

Western society takes massive quantities of drugs, of course: chemicals prescribed by physicians to shore up unhealthy bodies, to force sleep upon anxious minds, to yank the depressed from their troubled depths. Yet no one is permitted to take drugs for fun or for the purpose of gaining insight and wisdom. Young people have no cultural framework into which they can fit their legitimate needs for such experiences. As a result, drug taking acquires an aura of illegality and immorality, making it even more attractive. In addition, with no adult guidance leading them through the experience, young people must fend for themselves, sharing their experiences secretly and without thoughtful counsel.

Addiction: Plea From a Hungry Body and Soul

The greatest fear of most parents is that their children will become addicted to drugs, and the first casual puff of marijuana is seen as beginning the irreversible descent into heroin addiction. In addition, society now classifies addiction (to alcohol, at least) as a disease, as if it were the product of a viral agent or congenital defect, without participation by the addict's conscious mind.

All addiction is psychological. The dependence on a crutch, or the surrendering of personal power to a substance, begins as the need to fill a void in the psyche. Addiction can later assume physical qualities, masking the psyche's need as a physical need, the better to avoid introspective searching for the source of one's discontent.

Hiding deep beneath most substance addiction is the long-suppressed awareness that some plant substances foster dissolution of the ego and reunion with cosmic oneness. Drug addicts are almost always unhappy with some aspect of their lives, if not with life in general, and seek to dissolve the unhappy ego and restore the bliss of cosmic unity. Yet any drug's effect eventually wears off, and the ego is restored to supremacy. Because the addict rarely makes any genuine effort to improve his or her life conditions, after the drug's effect tapers off the misery returns unabated.

Just as wild animals kept in captivity will continue expressing behaviors which are appropriate in the wild but have no purpose in confinement, so does the addict perform an anachronistic ritual of ego dissolution and reunion with cosmic oneness, without the requisite social structure and sacramental basis for the experience. Stripped of the ritualistic context in which the use of psychoactive drugs is an appropriate and socially validated experience, the addict "goes through the motions," like a confined chicken futilely scratching its wire cage, acting out a behavior which offers no permanent relief or improvement because no social framework guides the experience.

Another factor to consider in western addiction is that either a manmade chemical compound or a highly refined extract from a plant source is used. Cocaine, for example, is the highly refined residue of the coca plant. Just as taking synthetically derived vitamin supplements in no way matches the health-giving qualities of vitamins embedded in fresh fruits and vegetables, so does refining a psychoactive substance out of its parent plant eliminate many mediating and balancing chemical partners which aid the body's assimilation of the psychoactive element. These "companion elements" act as buffers or enhancers, depending upon the body's size and health, adjusting the psychoactive element's effect on the ingester's system. Both overdose and below-threshold effects are minimized by these companion elements.

When the psychoactive substance is refined out of the parent plant, these mediating effects are lost. The plant's intelligence in moderating its effect upon the human body is lost. What is left is a powerful and potentially dangerous substance taken in pure form, forced upon the body without buffers to mediate the experience.

The use of crack cocaine among the inner city poor is perhaps the ultimate expression of how drug use has been cheapened and prostituted in your culture. The parent plant is stripped of its mind-altering element, then it and its intelligence discarded; the refined extract offers a flash of release from a decaying, chaotic social system; and the ritual lighting of the powder and subsequent high are the pathetic caricature of ancestral rituals welcoming the visions and wisdom offered by the plant world's teachers.

Bad Drugs vs. Good Drugs: Tools of the System

Many point out the apparent hypocrisy of society's banning certain drugs while allowing other potent mind-altering substances—nicotine and alcohol, for example—to be sold in every corner store. Comparing the statistics between the devastating effects of alcohol—lost productivity, drunken driving, broken families, and so on—versus the minimal social effects of marijuana, why then does society permit one and ban the other?

For the capitalist system to function, the ruling class needs a large pool of complacent, uncomplaining workers who willingly sacrifice their own fulfillment and family life in order to serve the system by performing repetitive, mindless tasks. The present system could not survive in a culture of conscious individuals whose highest priorities were relationships, meaningful work, and personal growth. The system persists only because so many willingly work as drones in order to achieve a baseline level of comfort and security.

Alcohol is a depressant; it dulls the mind and body. It prevents clear thought, purposeful action, and introspective searching. In short, it is the perfect drug to offer in unlimited quantities to workers whose minds must be dulled from thinking too clearly and sharply about their condition and the system in which they are trapped. The custom of heading straight from work for the bar is the ruling class's dream routine: for rather than protesting the inhuman nature of the work they do, workers drown the cries from their anguished souls in the quick poison of a shot glass. The system also subtly encourages the use of alcohol as a symbol of rebellion among the young and disenfranchised, for what true rebellion can grow from a sedated, comatose populace?

Mushrooms, peyote, LSD, Ecstasy, ayahuasca: now these are truly dangerous drugs! They lift the mind above the mundane everyday world into realms of greater wisdom and awareness; they expose the lie of separation on which the system is built; they restore a sense of life purpose loftier than owning a home; they foster direct experience of the unity of all life; they encourage the user to pursue spiritual growth and loving relationships as higher goals than economic stability; they offer glimpses of eternal life after physical death.

What threats to the system! What would happen to the economic juggernaut paving over the earth if suddenly everyone placed family, enlightenment, and personal growth as higher priorities than making a living? If everyone understood the unity of all life and protested the destruction of the natural world as the necessary price of "progress"? If everyone dropped their tribal and national allegiances and bonded in one global family?

The system allows drugs which fracture, sedate, and suppress consciousness. It bans drugs which enhance, stimulate, and expand consciousness. That is the sole criterion.

Just Say Yes—Occasionally

If the outcome of the present ecological crisis allows continued human presence on the earth, it follows that a new worldview, a new approach to life, will be necessary to ensure long-term survival. Most likely this will take the shape of a nature-based cosmology, one in which the laws of nature are followed as the basis for human law. Also, the pre-Christian understanding that all of nature is alive and suffused with consciousness, purpose, and meaning, must be restored.

When the human race once again assumes its welcome place in the natural order, and a respect and appreciation for the vegetable kingdom without which human life is impossible is renewed, man may well return to cherishing his plant teachers for the visions and wisdom they offer. In such a context—in a sacred, respectful, socially validated context—the ingestion of plant teachers strengthens and balances human society, softening the dangerous potentials latent in man's rational focus. To this millennia-old, traditional, sacred use of psychoactive plants, we can only Just Say Yes.

The Mind-Body Connection

It would be helpful to begin at the beginning, with an understanding of how the body is created and sustained at an energetic level. For the body is truly "spirit made flesh" in that it is sustained by a grid of energy and consciousness which shapes its form and sustains it with a flow of life-sustaining vitality.

Imagine a membrane separating the physical dimension as you experience it and the vast unseen realms of consciousness which lie outside the reach of your senses. In truth, this membrane simply demarcates the vibrational boundary between your senses' scope and the swarms of consciousness escaping their detection. All dimensions interpenetrate and overlap each other; pure consciousness does not exist in some distant "place," but simply vibrates at a frequency above your senses' perception, even as it swarms about you.

Every living being springs from a vibrational blueprint, a matrix of design and intent which pulses into physical expression by decelerating to frequencies compatible with matter. Every minute particle of the body is sustained by a corresponding point of energy in its nonphysical blueprint. The blueprint is much more than a carbon copy of the body, for it contains within its totality all possible configurations of the body's growth from conception to old age. In your time terms, the body's growth from birth to maturity is guided by manipulating the flows of energy from the blueprint into form. Each "energy point" in the blueprint can be thought of as a spigot, which is turned on and off throughout life as the body's changing condition warrants. By turning such energy-spigots on and off, and directing the intensity of their energetic flow, the higher self molds its body along its life journey.

Each different organ and system of the body springs from a distinct vibrational pattern in the nonphysical blueprint. Blood coursing through vein, bone and muscle, heart and spleen, all originate as discrete matrices of energy nestled within the blueprint; when thrust into physicality, they form the smoothly functioning, integrated systems of the body. The result is that each organ and system carries a distinct frequency and pattern of vibration; each "sings" a unique song. This has profound implications for the future of healing.

The physical system rides a fundamental binary pulsation during which energy is thrust from the nonphysical realm into physical form, and then flows back from the material side to the nonphysical. As the system blinks "on," *vitalizing energy* flows into the physical domain; as it blinks "off," *information* returns to the realm of pure consciousness. The perpetual incoming flow of vitalizing energy is what sustains the system's myriad life forms. In turn, the reversal flow of information apprises the bodies of consciousness participating in the system of the experiences gathered by their physical offshoots. Back and forth, on and off, in a two-way flow of energy and information, the physical system is sustained.

The reversal flow of information is crucial because the fundamental law of the earth system is freedom of thought and will, and learning the power of thought in creating experience. If the blueprint thrust itself into physicality in unblemished purity irrespective of the body's experiences, no results would seem to accrue from behavioral choices made: one could abuse and maim the body without apparent effect, for in the next "blink" it would be restored whole. By receiving a constant flow of information from the body and mind as to choices made and experiences garnered, the blueprint is altered accordingly, absorbing the effects of thought and behavior into the body's subsequent expression. A lasting scar, a tattoo, a lost limb—all will be woven into the blueprint as alterations in its energetic patterns and carried forward into future expression.

❖   ❖   ❖

The impact of thought on the body's health and longevity is just now beginning to be seriously examined by western science. Working from its materialist model, where consciousness is considered incapable of affecting matter, the influence of mind on the body has long been dismissed. At the other extreme are those who contend that the body is entirely under the control of the mind and that through sufficient force of will and intent, one should be able to heal any ailment and live forever. The truth, of course, lies somewhere in between.

Once it is recognized that the body is itself a grid of vitalized energy—essentially consciousness thickening into form—the formerly rigid boundary between mind and body dissolves. However, it is important to recognize the distinction between mind and body: the body vibrates at a much slower frequency than the mind, and is molded by its blueprint, whereas the mind operates at a much accelerated frequency and is largely free of externally imposed design.

Just as nerve pathways carry information between the brain and the body's far reaches, so are there vibrational pathways through which a much richer exchange between mind and body flows. The body is exquisitely sensitive to changes in mood and mind, altering its chemical and hormonal balances with every fleeting thought. Still, there are limits to the effect mind and body have on each other, for the vast difference in vibrational frequency limits the resonance of their communication, and the body receives its primary direction from its blueprint, not the mind.

These limits to mind-body synchrony work to your benefit: they prevent the body from collapsing at every dark thought. It takes a habitual, long-term pattern of thought to affect the body, for the mind does not directly affect the body; it affects the body's *blueprint*, which in turn alters the body's expression. As consciousness sweeps back across the membrane to the nonphysical realm, any consistent pattern of thought will gradually permeate the fields of energy sustaining the blueprint.

As an example, if you consider old age to be a certain misery of chronic pain and debility, as the years pass the mind's thought pattern affects the energy flowing from the spigot of each energy point, gradually constricting its flow, reducing the stream of life-sustaining vitality and producing the self-fulfilling prophecy of a crippled, weary old body.

The reason mind and body share limited communication across the gulf of vibrational disparity is that, in the best of circumstances, *you need never give your body a moment's thought*. Your body's intent and purpose is to carry you safely and healthily through the adventures sought by your mind. Unless there are specific reasons for the body itself to become the focal point of experience, its intent is to purr efficiently as the mind's unheralded valet. The body's intent is not to instantly and perfectly reflect the mind's fluid flow of consciousness, but to facilitate the mind's quest for experience. If the body always reflected the mind's thoughts with perfect fidelity, it would become an equal partner, forcing the mind to focus on the body's fluctuating condition. The body's purpose is to remain a background aide, not an equal partner.

This relationship is enforced by limiting the communication between mind and body to a constant appraisal of each other's condition and the body's gradual expression of chronic thought patterns. This compromise between the body's instantaneous reflection of the mind's thoughts and a rigid divorce between the two ensures that the body is free from having to mirror wild mood swings or brief depression, while it will faithfully reflect any chronic, habitual thought pattern, whether salutary or detrimental. So the truth of the mind-body connection lies between the extremes of absolute synchrony and complete divorce.

❖   ❖   ❖

American culture's preoccupation with the body—with health and illness, diet and nutrition, fitness and longevity—reflects a larger social condition, the accelerating unraveling of the cultural fabric. To live, to thrive, one must feel a sense of power and control over one's life and one's surroundings. During times of social upheaval, when it seems that effort and honesty go unrewarded, that a tide of madness laps ever higher at the cultural gates, and that nothing one does can right the listing ship of state, each person's circle of power contracts. The simultaneous unraveling of institutional systems—education, medicine, the economy, government, etc.—overwhelms individual initiative and effort; to feel any power and control at all, one must narrow one's "zone of influence" to family, home, and body.

Also driving the obsession with the body is the fear and denial of death. Whatever one's spiritual leaning, teachings about the realms beyond death's door remain unprovable conjecture until the actual passing, and those who have made the crossing are largely mute (with a few exceptions!). Westerners have the unpalatable choice between Christianity's heaven-and-hell-with-purgatory-on-the-side scheme, or science's cold extinction of consciousness at death. The first offends reason, the other the spirit; so death looms as an inexplicable mystery. Naturally, one seeks to postpone as long as possible plunging into such a dark enigma!

A decaying social order and the fear of death are the primary motivators behind the obsession with the body, fitness, and longevity. If all is chaos, if death is a mysterious realm of unknown contour, then at least one may bring order and reliable result in shaping one's body and postponing its decay. The paradox is that you create what you fear—and when you *fear* the body's decay, when you *fear* death, you energize those potentials with greater vitality than they would otherwise have. It is not an act itself, but the intent behind it, that determines its meaning and effect. When you act out of fear, you bring the feared experience that much closer to realization.

The fitness obsession also indicates how estranged mind and body have become in your culture. A normal, healthy symbiosis between mind and body means the body transmits its needs and desires to the mind, which acknowledges and acts upon those impulses. No body on earth would choose to run a 26-mile marathon, or endure a triathalon, or struggle in oxygen-starved panic to a mountaintop miles above the earth. That these activities are considered evidence of "fitness" underscores the depth of the divorce between mind and body. The wanton disrespect for the body which drives such activities can only come back to haunt the perpetrator in later years, for the mind's abuse of the body is like a parent abusing a child, with the same long-term consequences.

The issue is one of *intent*—is the motivating force behind an exercise regimen one of love for the body, cherishing its strength and vitality; or is it fear and contempt? It is the intent behind any fitness routine that determines its long-lasting effects, not the workout itself.

By the same token, the realm of food and nutrition is often clouded by fear, especially fear for the body's imagined frailty. The body is considered by many to be a fragile china doll, easily damaged and broken. Strict dietary regimens are followed lest the body crumble under an onslaught of free radicals, "bad" cholesterol, and toxic pesticides.

The hallmark of the human species is its *adaptability*. Reason grants you the freedom to live anywhere on the planet, under any conditions, and to take advantage of whatever nutritional offerings are available—from the whale blubber of the great white north to the tropical fruits of the equator. The human body is eminently adaptable, designed with an innate flexibility which supports its peripatetic species. The body delights in the natural world's overflowing cornucopia of diverse foods. When this natural abundance is unnaturally restricted due to personal or religious prohibitions, the body suffers some diminished vitality.

Any food is more than its vitamins and minerals and roughage; for every living being is suffused with consciousness. Eating a freshly picked fruit or a freshly killed animal brings that being's consciousness, to a limited extent, into the body, there to nourish and vitalize the cells not only with nutrients but with vital life energy. Just as your mind craves a diversity of experience, so does the body crave and benefit from ingesting as wide a variety of food sources as possible.

When the body's natural desire for food diversity is denied due to dietary proscriptions invented by the mind, again a disrespect for the body creeps into the relationship. If a strict diet is intended to enhance longevity, prevent cancer, avoid fat and cholesterol, or boost vitamin C, beneath these motives lies a deeper disrespect for the body's adaptability, flexibility, and thirst for diversity. This only further estranges body from mind.

Again, the key is not the foods ingested, but the motivating intent behind nutritional choices. In the deepest sense, wolfing down a fast-food cheeseburger and soft drink without a thought to their effect on the body is healthier than a strict macrobiotic diet followed out of fear for the body's frail susceptibility to impure foods. This is not to say that a long-term diet of high-fat, low-fiber foods carries no deleterious effects, or that those effects can be entirely mitigated by proper mental attitude. The point is that one's perspective on diet affects not only the immediate impact of a meal on the body, but also carries long-term effects on the body's nonphysical blueprint.

If we may momentarily revert to a dualistic framework, consider that the body is both an organism operating within the laws and limitations of nature, and is affected by its owner's mental activity. If you swallow a large dose of arsenic, no amount of Zen-inspired clarity will override the poison's lethal certainty. A lifelong diet of high-fat, low-fiber foods washed down with alcohol is certainly more challenging for the body to process and derive adequate nutrition from than a diet high in grains and vegetables. These effects do operate on a purely organismic level. At the same time, however, the body receives a constant stream of thought and belief pouring from the mind, with long-term attitudes etched into the body's blueprint as well. This ineluctably affects the body's overall health and harmony.

So the healthiest diet is one which combines foods the body easily and efficiently processes with a lenient, open-minded and -mouthed embrace of the world's great culinary diversity. A slice of cheesecake or pizza, eaten out of occasional zesty indulgence rather than guilt, enhances overall mental and physical health in a way that a strict regimen of rice and beans cannot.

Because humanity's purpose is to rise above the purely nature-based focus of most animal species and to engage the world through reason and symbol, the human body is designed to require minimal food to sustain good health. This frees humanity from the constant foraging compelling most animal species. In order to achieve this efficiency, the human body is designed as an axis, a long, lean pole, which is nature's most efficient design. A tight engine of flesh and muscle encasing a multijointed, compact skeleton allows for maximum exploration and creative expression sustained by a minimum of food-gathering activity.

The body you know is but one of the various fields of energy anchored at the spine; it is the most slowly vibrating of the various human "bodies." The other bodies, which whir at frequencies beyond your senses' reach, are engaged in probing your environment, exchanging information with others at the auric level, and tuning into the vast realms of information swarming about the planet. These energetic bodies are designed to operate within a certain distance from the spine, depending on their frequency and purpose.

These two aspects of the human body—its highly efficient axis-like design and its unseen energetic fields—bear on the issue of obesity. Is prejudice against overweight people an unfair and unwarranted intolerance, or does it have some deeper basis?

On both counts, being overweight impairs the healthy functioning of the body and full realization of its potential. If the human form is designed as a lean, efficient axis, then any significant deviation from this blueprint impairs its functioning at peak efficiency. This is obvious enough: overweight people have greater difficulty in moving about, playing sports, maintaining muscle tone, and so on. To a lesser or greater extent, this limits options and diminishes full embrace of life's potentials.

Perhaps a more deleterious effect of obesity, though unseen and unrecognized, is its interference with the smooth functioning of the body's energetic fields. These fields operate within a standard distance from the spine and do not expand to compensate for obesity. If a field is meant to operate within a foot of the spine, and that area is filled with flesh rather than air, the field's performance is impaired: it can neither operate at peak efficiency nor offer the highest quality information to the subconscious mind. The greater a body's corpulence, the more the energetic fields are forced to operate inside the body rather than beyond it, and their efficiency and clarity are commensurately impaired. Thus the prejudice against obesity is not merely a cultural defect, but springs from a deeper recognition that obese individuals are violating the intent and design of the species' form and suffer clouded communion with the world at large as a result of their impaired energy fields.

That said, it is increasingly common knowledge that lying beneath the struggle with obesity is often a struggle with feelings of self-worth and self-love. Since the primal, the original experience of love was feeding at mother's breast, the equation "food is love" is writ deeply in the human psyche and is often reverted to in times of stress and wounds to the ego. Mother's breast is no longer available, but the mere act of eating replicates, in crude caricature, that original experience of food as love and serves as balm on a wounded soul.

To truly heal the challenge of obesity, one must look beyond fad diets and crash fasting, and restore the deep inner sense of love and worth that came automatically at mother's breast. It is no coincidence that this issue should be so prominent today as the race makes a halting transition from an age of external validation—including a religion based on a external God, a school system based on competition and performance, and an economy based on competitive capitalism—toward an age of internal validation, based on awareness of each person's innate divinity, and cooperation and mutual interdependence in the social sphere.

Naturally, this transition plays out at the microscopic level in each individual's struggle with self-worth and self-love. Those struggling with obesity play out the larger cultural transition in graphic terms: Am I a divine, lovable, and worthy person just for existing, or must I have external validation of my worth? Do I find sources of approval and recognition from within, or must I subliminally seek mother's unconditional love through food substitutes? While those grappling with obesity play out this psychodrama most personally and dramatically, they also serve as symbols for the larger culture, where everyone struggles with these issues. Thus the ultimate "cure" for obesity is self-love, self-worth, and self-validation— and a culture founded on respect for the innate divinity of every being.

Men, Women and Love:
Toward a New Understanding

The recently emerging men's movement, a counterpoint to the decades-old women's movement, brings to the forefront of social awareness the eternal questions of the nature of masculinity and femininity; to what extent the roles and qualities traditionally ascribed to either sex are innate or culturally imposed; whether romantic love is the highest form of bond between the sexes; and everyone's favorite subject, human sexuality.

In this time of great social upheaval and change, as the old order crumbles to make way for the new, these fundamental questions and issues naturally float to the surface of awareness, for their expression in any culture is the bedrock foundation on which are built all other social edifices. Let us take a look, then, at these eternally fascinating and perplexing issues: what it means to be a man, a woman, to join in partnership, to make love.

The Great Divide

The human species, for all its great diversity, arises from a single pool of consciousness, which might be termed the "human pool." This pool exists on a level of pure consciousness as a vast, amorphous pool of intent, that intent being to animate the physical beings playing out the vast sweep of human history. This pool, as it descends levels of vibration to vitalize beings at the level of physical matter, fragments and splinters into increasingly fine focuses of intent, weaving the patterns of human diversity: the two sexes, the great races, and so on. Each person born carries certain "imprints" based on the race, sex, culture, and historical period chosen; these provide the background consciousness coloring a person's experience.

Any great division must be made for a purpose; such divisions always signify that a certain trait or quality will be emphasized by one strand while other qualities will be the focus of another. Just as nature is strongest when most diverse, so is human consciousness healthiest when its innumerable potentials are distributed among the great divisions of human consciousness. The ultimate purpose is balance, as we shall see when we discuss love and sex.

Given this understanding, it naturally flows that men and women are fundamentally different; that the division of consciousness lying behind the creation of two sexes implies that each carries a unique purpose or quality. If you consider what you are for a moment, you see yourself as a physical being animated by consciousness. This most fundamental quality of human existence—matter animated by spirit—is the basis of the two sexes.

Woman: Spiritual Guardian of Earth

To woman falls the mantle of spiritual guardian of the earth. This means that woman's primary psychological coloration is spiritual; that matters of the heart, of love, of connection, of drawing together, are her most natural qualities.

If a woman's nature is essentially spiritual, meaning that she dwells primarily in the realm of consciousness, by looking at consciousness we can understand how woman's qualities naturally flow from it. Pure consciousness, divorced from matter, has a tendency to "rise up" to ever greater levels;

at each higher level, discrete units of consciousness are bonded to form great masses of energy. There is less and less division into distinct blocks of consciousness as one rises to higher realms. Just as human consciousness at its highest is an amorphous, united pool of consciousness, so then does human consciousness join with all plant and animal consciousness to form an even higher "earth consciousness," and so on.

So if woman's focus is primarily spiritual, reflecting the qualities of consciousness, she has a natural tendency to "draw together," to include, to open her arms wide and embrace the different, the small, the weak and helpless. Women predominate in the helping professions as teachers, social workers, nurses, and volunteers, because these provide outlets for the feminine qualities of love, comfort, and aid.

The most obvious expression of woman's nurturance is that she bears children. Young human children are so helpless for so long that they require years of constant love, affection, and gentle guidance to become happy, healthy members of the clan. Young children live primarily in the realm of consciousness—rational thought and physical mastery come later—and it naturally falls to woman, who shares the young child's spiritual nature, to nurture the species' young. You know the humorous phrase—"a face only a mother could love"—and recognize the truth behind it, that a mother pays scant attention to the physical wrapping on the child's soul, focusing instead on the spirit itself.

Woman is slow to commit violence, to join men in their eternal blood baths over territory, power, and wealth. Even a woman deeply proud of her cultural tribe feels a common bond with the "enemy," hears their hearts being in synchrony with hers, knows they love their children as she loves hers. So woman largely removes herself from masculine violence, unable to shake off the innate spiritual bond she shares with others.

Man: Material Keeper of Earth

You are consciousness embodied in physical form. As woman is aligned with your spiritual nature, to man falls the focus of material mastery and manipulation. Man's emphasis is on structure, form, reason, logic, creation, destruction, and power as defined in terms of wealth and territory. While woman gazes inward, toward the heart and soul, man gazes firmly outward, into the physical medium.

The overarching masculine theme is the dynamic play of creation and destruction. Like exuberant children building sand castles and kicking them over, man focuses his energy on creating ever more elaborate, detailed, intricate, and complex structures, then either destroying them or (preferably) destroying someone else's. This is true both in terms of physical structures—buildings, temples, and so forth—and in human institutions such as government, business, and religion. The focus is on creation of new forms on the dust of the old.

When an invader conquers new territory, the invasion is frequently accompanied by massive destruction of extant structures, particularly temples or other spiritual sites—witness China's ongoing pillaging of Tibet. Because man's focus is outward, the urge is to destroy the physical expressions of other cultures and to impose one's own. What is not understood is that culture flows from the heart and spirit, and these cannot be crushed by bulldozers and bombs.

While creation is considered a positive act and destruction a negative one, in truth they are inextricably linked in the eternal dynamic of creation-and-destruction. For new forms to be built, the old must be swept away. Nature operates in this fashion; the soil which grows your food was once giant boulders of rock, "destroyed" through glaciation and weathering. While nature is often considered feminine, in this sense nature's processes are more closely aligned with the masculine, with the cycle of birth and death, creation and destruction.

Because man's focus is on physical expression, there is a greater variety of personality types, talents, intelligence, and pathology than among women. Woman is aligned with your spiritual source, a constant flow of energy which provides a steady bedrock foundation. Man is less influenced by this foundation, and therefore splashes out into the physical medium in greater variety: saint and sinner, killer and healer, genius and idiot, commando and pastor, gentle elder and ruthless dictator. The boundaries of human expression are broader for men than for women, as a general rule. The overwhelming preponderance of male names writ large in luminous artistic, scientific, and engineering achievements throughout history cannot be attributed to sexist culture alone.

Men and Women: Electrifying Magnetism

After the blissful ignorance of childhood, where the opposite sex is ignored if not scorned, puberty triggers a powerful attraction which will color the whole of adult life. Why, alone among the animals, should the human urge toward romance and sex be a year-round affair? What purpose does the compelling urge to join in romantic/sexual union serve?

Our focus for this discussion is on the auric field, for this is the energetic body involved whenever you share close proximity with another. From six feet away, your auric field and those of others begin to overlap and to exchange information, transmitted as units of electromagnetic energy. The auric field holds recent memories, the nature of your thoughts, and information about your reincarnational history. This information is freely exchanged, without the obfuscation and dissembling available to you in verbal exchanges, whenever your auric field overlaps with another.

When you are repulsed by someone, what do you do? You back away, refusing to allow them into your field. When you love someone, what do you do? You want to be near them, to hold them, hug them, cuddle them, make love to them. The compulsion you feel to touch and embrace is driven by the auric field's urge to exchange information of as high a quality and fidelity as possible, to literally absorb the other's essence into your own.

To return our discussion to romance, remember that the purpose of creating divisions in consciousness is strength through diversity, stability through balance. When two individuals of disparate qualities join, they create a gestalt of consciousness of greater strength and power than a single individual, however well-balanced, could achieve.

You are spirit housed in flesh. Woman is the spiritual guardian of earth; man is its material keeper. By joining these two disparate qualities, a synthesis—the couple—is formed. This synthesis is of greater psychological strength than a person alone can realize, for each absorbs from the other the quality lacking in oneself. Woman gains man's physical strength and stability; man gains woman's nurturance and spiritual outlook.

This exchange is not so much verbal or the built-up accretion of shared experience, but occurs at the auric level as a constant blending of energy in which each absorbs what is needed from the other and offers what the other needs. Many healings of incipient illness take place among couples, with neither knowing it. Angers, frustrations, and disappointments can be melted away with the infusion of loving energy from a partner. That single people fall ill more often and die younger than couples is testament to this.

The basis of romantic attraction is thus an unconscious desire to achieve wholeness through synergy, balance through the blending of energies. One feels a lack, a void, an imbalance, and seeks to right it by joining with a partner offering the missing quality. This leads us to—

Human Sexuality

The driving force behind the sexual urge is, in truth, not the need to procreate, but the desire to *incorporate*. By joining with a partner who offers qualities lacking in oneself during a free-flowing, spontaneous, highly energetic encounter of skin against skin, each encourages the maximum acceleration of energy in the other, allowing the greatest exchange of vibrational energy and information. Sex is the most pleasurable, dynamic act you know, and the vibrant waves of ecstasy ripple to all higher "bodies." Thus is the deepest purpose of sex— energy exchange—fulfilled.

Notice how sexual activity is often quasi-cannibalistic, with active use of the tongue and mouth on the body of the partner. This underscores that sex's purpose is to incorporate, as you figuratively "eat" the body of the other, or literally insert one body into another.

The difference between male and female approaches to sexuality is a source of constant puzzlement and misunderstanding. The woman is exasperated by the man's insistence on getting to the point with a minimum of forestalling pleasantries, while the man must abide the woman's need for cuddling and loving words. Knowing the fundamental difference between the sexes—spirit and physicality—it naturally flows that sex should be an emotional, spiritual experience for women, while for men it is more a physical act, done and forgotten.

These differences are exacerbated in western culture, as dangerously unbalanced as it is. A healthy culture balances male and female energies, spirit and reason, into a smooth symbiosis in which both qualities are equally revered and employed in navigating a healthy course. As western culture has for millennia favored man's materially based approach and disdained woman's spirituality, the culture as a whole staggers forward on one leg. Each individual man reflects this imbalance as well; and the desperate need for balance, for an infusion of spiritual warmth and healing, drives man to the sole socially acceptable outlet: sex with woman. That men have "only one thing on their minds" is true only in your unbalanced culture, where the profound void men feel can be filled only in the arms of woman.

Homosexuality and Other Perversions

Woke you up, didn't we?

If the purpose of sex is to achieve balance through the synergetic blending of male and female energies, what of homosexuality? Is this a perversion, a crude blunting of healthy sexual expression due to childhood trauma or personal choice?

The eternal question of when homosexuality is imprinted can never be answered by your culture as long as it emphasizes matter over consciousness and allows no possibility of life choices being made before birth. For that is when homosexuality is chosen— before birth—by a soul desiring a certain flavor to a lifetime experience.

Remember that balance and stability are achieved through diversity; the greater the variety, the more stable the culture. From the first, homosexuality has been set up as part of the human species as a "laboratory" in which the male-female dynamic is distilled and focused into a single body, rather than the more common twosome. That is, while heterosexuals require a partner to achieve the balance and stability of male-female blending, homosexuals carry both energies within their psyches. Just as one can choose before birth to experience poverty, discrimination, wealth or power, one can also choose to participate in this ongoing experiment of blending the two great strands of human diversity within a single body.

This is not to say that homosexuals do not need life partners and sexual activity as much as anyone else. The drive is still there—to blend energies with another and achieve balance and harmony and healing, and to enjoy the sheer pleasure of sex. But there is a qualitative difference in homosexual activity, for two relatively "complete" individuals share their energies with each other, rather than a man and woman seeking to fill their respective voids.

Homosexuality is present in every time and culture as an ongoing distillation of the male-female dynamic, like a mirror reflecting back to straight society the condition of its male-female relations. It should be no surprise that balanced, harmonious cultures—such as Native American tribes—held special reverence for their homosexuals, while dangerously unbalanced cultures such as yours despise their gay brethren. They reflect back to you your own cultural and sexual imbalance.

Briefly, what of genuine perversions, sexual attraction toward children, animals, and the like? The easiest way to understand them is to recognize that the sex drive is the drive to incorporate. What qualities has the desired object or person? In the case of children, the quality is innocence, an innocence of adult romantic entanglements and the dangers they hold for rejection and humiliation. Those so frightened by such potential rejection may turn to persons who offer no such chance of rejection—children. To molest children is a desperate bid to incorporate their innocence, to flee from adult relationship and return to mother's unqualified love and acceptance.

Men & Women: The Future

Whenever a culture thrashes about in a sudden and profound shift of values and cultural worldview—as now occurs in western culture—the first grasping efforts at establishing a new order may, at times, be crude, exaggerated, self-righteous, or downright silly. Those in the vanguard of cultural change are ripping chunks from the future, trying to fashion them into a new cultural framework, and their efforts will necessarily be inchoate and raw.

Both the women's and men's movements now exhibit these symptoms. Suddenly "the Goddess" is everywhere, and claims are made that once there lived goddess-worshipping cultures in which men and women were equals in all things, the earth was revered, and life was bliss. The men's movement has events where men assume animal form and behavior, run around naked, connect with their "wild" selves, and drum for hours.

These are all valid, groping attempts at forging new masculine and feminine paradigms, the foundation of a new male-female dynamic. As is often the case, both movements reach into the distant past, dredging up atavistic tokens of long-vanished cultural practices, and with these threads attempt to weave a new cultural foundation.

The intent is true and worthy, the excess and silliness to be expected. But let us move past these incipient efforts at forging new sexual identities and dynamics, and explore the ultimate outcome of these efforts: how male and female identities will be shaped once the new order is realized. We return to our opening material: man is the material keeper of the earth, woman its spiritual guardian.

Man has strayed the farthest from his role, for men are now the political, corporate, and scientific leaders who lead the lemmings' march to ecological catastrophe. Gone is the connection between man and earth, the sense of caretaking, nurturing, and partnership with nature. As nature's eternal process of creation and destruction mirrors man's quality of building and destroying, it is man, not woman, whose activities most closely align with nature's. So the man of the future will restore his kinship with the natural world, will reassume the role of careful and loving steward of the earth. This will flow from a respect for nature as mirroring man's inner quality, and the recognition that nature magnifies this quality on a scale and with a perfection no human mind could fashion.

Man's need to be with nature is now twisted into violent expressions like hunting, fishing, and dirt bike racing. The man of the future will be fulfilled simply being with nature. Men need contact with wild places, where nature's creation/destruction dynamic plays unchecked by human hands, resonating with man's deepest quality. And every man should have a garden, both as an expression of partnership with nature and to restore the "provider" sensibility with an activity more tangible and satisfying than bringing home a paycheck.

If we offer the mantle of "spiritual guardian" to woman, such is not meant to shackle her to the limited sphere of kitchen-and-kids of yesteryear. Rather, it is to highlight the importance of woman as a counterpoint, a balancing influence, on man's exuberant creation and destruction. Woman brings heart and nurturance to human activity which, without her influence, risks degrading into the male "progress at all costs" mentality which now plunders the earth.

It is not that woman's activities should be circumscribed, but that she should bring to them her especial qualities. Women working as corporate executives are heralded as evidence of "liberation," yet if women must become men with high heels to advance in the corporate world, they are failing to achieve true liberation, which is the infusion of their empathic and nurturing qualities into that spiritual vacuum. True equality is when the male question "Can we do it?" is balanced with the feminine influence, "Is it good for all involved?"

One of the most important contributions women will make in the future is to take the lead role in spiritual understanding and ritual. Such has been the jealously guarded province of men for millennia, with the predictable result that more energy is put into building hierarchy and codifying dogma than in seeking spiritual truth. As woman is the natural spiritual guardian of earth, she will rise to leadership in spiritual exploration, education, and practice. A woman-based spirituality will be short on hierarchy and rigid dogma, long on celebration and heart-based altruism. Future spiritual practice will be far more spontaneous, free-flowing, and inclusive, with woman at the helm and altar.

As for relations between the sexes, the current condition known as romantic love will evolve into a new form of partnership, one based more on mutual expectation and need than on exclusivity and the fantastical projection of perfection onto the loved one. In your imbalanced culture, a romantic partner is often expected to fill the many roles no longer adequately met by society at large: lover, confidant, friend, parent, priest. As men, in particular, evolve into healthier relationships with each other, the exclusive focus on woman as the provider of all emotional needs will diminish. Men and women will always need each other and benefit from long-term partnership, but romantic love—with its jealousy, exclusivity, and possessiveness—will evolve into a broader context with the couple at the center of a richly interwoven social network.

We are sketching a brief outline of male-female dynamics; subtleties and exceptions are necessarily lost. We may seem to be rigidly dividing humanity's material and spiritual qualities into the two sexes, with no chance of blending or balance within each private heart. Of course each person is an amalgam of male and female qualities, a blend of energies. The difference lies in emphasis; as a rule, women are the spiritual guardians, men the material keepers of earth. The difference is what makes the synergistic blending of male/female energies so enthralling, and compels you to seek balance in the arms of the other.

This we offer as the natural state of male and female energies, and the reason for the difference in emphasis. As the future restores balance to male-female relations and cherishes their unique qualities as equally valid and essential, so will society itself naturally move into harmony and balance within itself and in its relationship with the earth.

Gaia Bank & Trust:
Building a Natural Economy

Despite the euphoria over the recent collapse of communism in Europe and the embrace by some communist countries of market socialism, meaning a move toward capitalist principles, few discern the deeper meaning of these events or the hidden portents affecting the future of capitalist economies. Indeed, as the capitalist and communist frameworks are both built upon western culture's divorce from the natural order, both must ultimately fail. That communism has done so first demonstrates only that in principle and practice it represents a far deeper violation of natural law than capitalism. Let us now examine in detail the principles of the natural economy—meaning the precepts by which nature creates and handles energy, her "capital"—and contrast them with the principles of western culture's two main economic expressions, capitalism and communism.

The Origin of Natural Law

First, let us further explore our contention that any human enterprise violating natural principles must ultimately fail. Why should this be so? How can nature impose her principles on human activity? Can the human species not distance itself from its natural origins if it so chooses?

By "nature" we mean the fundamental universal principles underlying all of creation, to which all matter and consciousness are bound. In your system, these principles find expression as "laws of nature"; the earth symbolically expresses universal law in the workings of the natural world. When one understands how nature works, one opens a doorway to understanding the deeper truths, the fundamental laws, governing all realms of creation.

Underlying your experienced reality is a constant flow of energy from outside the space-time matrix, a pulsation which carries the blueprint for the physical system. This steady, eternal pulsation is the conduit through which consciousness seeds the physical realm; consciousness rides the pulsation into physical manifestation.

All creatures, whatever their degree of consciousness, ride securely atop this steady infusion of energy, which underlies and ensures the harmony of the natural world. The human species, granted its unique focus of reason and symbolic manipulation, has the power to stray from the flow of energy seeding the physical world, to violate the universal principles interwoven with the source energy. As every act begets a consequence, those consequences you term "negative" are feedback that the values driving a person's or culture's behavior are out of harmony with natural law. The universe urges you back toward harmony, back toward restoration with nature, by offering negative results accruing from a violative act. The further one strays from acting in consonance with universal principle—the deeper the violation of natural law—the more egregious the consequence. So does the universe reflect back to you, on private and collective levels, whether your values and deeds are in harmony with natural law or violate it.

The Principles of Nature's Economy

While energy and consciousness infuse every element of creation, from the electron's dance to the whirl of galaxies, for this discussion we will consider that the fundamental source of life energy for your world is that created by plants during photosynthesis. This energy is the basic building block of the food chain, upon which all living beings depend. As plant energy is the elemental thread of the web of life, it is the "capital" of nature's economy. With this understanding, we can explore the principles which govern the natural economy.

The first principle, while valid at the level of plants, is even more apparent at the subatomic level: energy is in constant motion. Modern physics has cast aside the notion of a bedrock world of granular building blocks coalescing into structures of ever greater size. Instead, the physical system is seen as fields of pulsating activity, waves and particles dancing in perpetual motion, weaving the fabric you perceive as a bedrock world and universe.

This fundamental principle of the physical system applies at all levels: energy must be free to flow in its natural course. Consider the consequences of unnaturally blocking energy's free flow—damming a river, repressing anger, arteriosclerosis—and one finds a negative result accruing, a clue that natural law has been violated.

In nature's economy, free-flowing plant energy is the foundation of every healthy ecosystem. Plants use the sun's energy to grow leaves, roots, flowers, and fruit, absorbing the sun's rays and transmuting its energy into the eternal cycle of birth, growth, and release. Upon release of physical form, a plant's stored energy is freed, eaten by animals or returning to the earth during decay. The sun's energy is never frozen into place during the plant's life cycle, never locked away unavailable for use by the plant or others. The sun's warm spark fuels a perpetual, free-flowing dance of energy.

The second principle of nature's economy is this: nature always seeks balance. Nature creates a bedrock foundation of balance upon which all the astonishing diversity of creation depends. Harmony ensues when all elements of a system are functioning smoothly, within their natural ranges of activity, with no one element so out of balance as to violate the smooth performance of the whole.

When you open the door of a warm house on a cold day, the temperatures balance, leaving a lukewarm house. When you mix red and yellow dyes, they balance, into orange. When the earth's plates grind against each other, the building pressure balances, into an earthquake. At every level of existence, from the electron exchange of chemical reactions, to the homeostasis sustaining mammalian form, to the imponderable sweep of the galaxies, nature always seeks balance.

The third principle of nature's economy may seem more philosophical than physical at first: every living being, plant or animal, is driven by the urge toward self-fulfillment. Nothing simply exists without purpose. The plant stretches toward the sun, the bird builds its nest, the child paints and sings, all driven by the unconscious but unquenchable urge to live, to grow, to find self-fulfillment, each within the contours of its creaturehood.

Each being is born a bundle of potential and spends its life striving to express and fulfill that potential as broadly and grandly as it can. While often reduced by western scientists to "instincts" like self-preservation and the avoidance of pain, every being is driven first and foremost by the urge toward self-fulfillment, the realization of its divine potential.

A corollary of this principle is that the highest harmony results when each being is free to pursue its private self-fulfillment without interference or control by others. You may marvel at the wondrous interwoven web of life in a given ecosystem, from a desert to an arctic plain to the ocean's depths, but no creature within these systems gives a moment's thought to sustaining the larger scheme in which it plays a part, and no overseer dictates how each shall live. The harmony arises spontaneously, seemingly miraculously, from each creature's pursuit of its own self-fulfillment.

The last law of nature's economy we will consider here is this: nature knows no surplus. The plant uses the sun's energy for growth and producing seed; it does not generate more chlorophyll than it can use. Each creature arises every morning needing to find its food anew; nature's creatures own no silos. Hibernating creatures build up fat to sustain them through the long winter, and squirrels bury their winter's cache, but neither is building surplus beyond what it needs to survive until spring, when daily foraging must resume.

If energy must remain in constant motion, surplus is a violation for it represents energy extracted from the perpetual dance, held apart from the ceaseless recycling of the natural world. No creature living in harmony with nature hoards more than it reasonably needs to survive; for every creature lives with a deep, unconscious faith and trust in nature's beneficence.

The Principles of Western Culture

Before focusing specifically on western culture's economic systems, let us take a broader look at the basic principles underlying all of western culture. For all realms of thought and activity—whether science, religion, politics, or economics—are built upon the foundation of western culture's core values, as a myriad of houses could be built upon a given foundation.

The overarching value driving western culture is that humanity is separated, even divorced, from nature. Western culture views itself as having stepped outside of the natural world and its guiding principles, and is freed from conducting itself in accordance with nature's plan. This core value permeates every aspect of western culture.

For example, while the Judeo-Christian heritage and scientific rationalism would claim no commonality with each other, both arise from the same foundation. The Genesis story posits a creator figure who creates the human species and then drives it from the Garden—divorcing it from nature—while also granting humanity dominion over nature, as if nature were an unruly child requiring constant supervision. Science's creation story has the universe originating in a tiny ball of matter—whose source is never revealed—which inexplicably explodes and spews the universe into being. Humanity is seen as the pinnacle of evolution's long march from primordial slime; thus man is "above" all other species. In both religious and scientific creation stories, then, humanity is separated from its spiritual source—either through misbehavior or because there is no such source—and is granted superiority over all other life forms. Both myths express the same core value.

Another core value of western culture, through which it filters experience, is the linear perspective. Nature works in cycles, spheres, loops, feedback, and balance. Western culture thinks and works in straight lines, right angles, boxes, and exponential growth. As an example, consider the housing created by cultures living in harmony with nature—the Eskimo's igloo, the Native American's tepee, the African tribe's thatched hut—all are built in a rounded or sloping shape, mimicking nature's spherical pattern, and allowing the free circulation of heat and air. Western culture, by contrast, lives in boxes with flat planes and right angles, in which dead air and heat are trapped in the corners. Western culture's linear perspective developed from its divorce from nature and her principles, resulting in structures—physical, theoretical, economic—which violate natural law.

The Principles of Human Economy

Understanding the core values of western culture as divorce from nature and a linear perspective, let us examine how these values lay the foundation on which western economics is built.

First, what is money? At base, human capital is identical to nature's capital: plant energy. As humanity progressed from nomadic tribes to agriculture, the entire tribe was no longer required to hunt and prepare food; those tending the crops could produce more than they needed, thus freeing some to engage in other labor. Currency arose as symbolic food which could be exchanged for real food as needed. Farmers grew more food than their families needed, freeing the town's other specialists—blacksmith, priest, mayor, doctor—to pursue their work, be paid in currency (symbolic food), and exchange the currency with the farmer for the real thing.

The same process holds true today: you work a job, are paid in currency, and exchange that currency for food. That there is money left over for other necessities and luxuries does not invalidate the principle that money is symbolic food; every groaning empty belly echoes this principle's truth. At base, then, both natural and human economies are built on the same foundation: "capital" is symbolic food, stored plant energy.

The basis of capitalism is private property, but does nature know private property? It is true that almost all creatures create private, inviolate spheres of control, often known as nests, which serve as a home base offering security from the elements and predators and a nursery for the young. Most creatures will defend their spheres of control vehemently, often violently, sometimes to the death. It seems, then, that nature's design includes the notion of private property to the extent of providing each creature a safe haven, which others may violate only at their peril.

While no one begrudges a human family its safe warm home, the massive accumulation of private property far beyond need or reason grinds against the conscience. Recognizing the violation of moral law which allows some to accumulate vast wealth while others starve, capitalist countries evolve governmental structures and laws which seek to redistribute, through taxation and social programs, the excess property holdings of the rich. While the impulse is noble and in harmony with nature's guiding principle of balancing extremes, we must look deeper and ask why anyone would want to accumulate such vast holdings, why anyone would live with the acquisition of property as one's central life purpose.

We must look to the spiritual life of western culture, or what remains of it. Unlike native cultures, which recognize the spirituality of all creation, western culture drained the natural world of spiritual content when it dispensed with the gods of Greek and Roman mythology and installed one omniscient God high in the heavens, standing apart from His creation as a sculptor regards his clay. Believing in an omniscient, all-powerful creator figure fosters a sense of childish impotence, as this particular creator figure is given to fits of pique and flooding the globe when displeased, among other deadly eccentricities. The earth is no longer regarded as host to innumerable swarms of consciousness, manifesting in sky and water and tree, but is seen as a cold, indifferent bed of rock upon which one lives under the unblinking gaze of a capricious creator in whose hands lies the power of destruction and eternal condemnation. More, the individual no longer feels the flow of spirituality through himself and all creation, but stands meaningless and empty without validation from above.

In addition, as traditional religion has lost its grasp and given way to the ascendence of reason and science, many are left with no spiritual life whatsoever. This total divorce from spiritual truth triggers a quiet terror, an existential insecurity, in the face of a random existence without design or purpose and the belief in physical death as the cessation of consciousness.

The intrinsic urge toward self-fulfillment, toward realization of one's highest potential, is blunted and perverted in such a culture. The urge to fulfill oneself, one's talents, one's dreams, is rendered either irrelevant by the capricious creator or pointless by living on a cold sphere whirling in an empty void. Blunted from healthy expression—fulfilling oneself in the security of a world pulsing with spirituality immanent in all things—the urge toward self-fulfillment is perverted into two extremes: the relinquishing of all worldly possessions in the hope of currying favor with the creator for a blissful after-life, as in taking a vow of poverty; or the frantic accumulation of property and possessions as the only standard of worth in a world without meaning.

It is noteworthy that the two superpowers, one a bastion of capitalism, the other of communism, explicitly divorced economic and political life from spiritual life. The American Constitution decrees the separation of church from state, while the Soviet Union banned religious practice altogether. This cements in the very foundation of modern economic life the absolute divorce of spiritual truth from economic practice.

The Principles of Capitalism

Let us examine capitalism more closely and compare its principles with those of nature's economy. By doing so we can determine the extent to which it violates natural law and understand the potential for its ultimate success or demise.

Capitalism does embrace nature's fundamental law that every being must be free to pursue its self-fulfillment without interference or restriction. By allowing each person to accumulate wealth in his name and for his benefit, capitalism upholds this fundamental law. The problem arises when, because of the spiritual emptiness of western culture, the accumulation of wealth becomes the sole standard of meaning, leading to violation of other natural principles.

First, each person is free to accumulate far more than he could ever spend, in one lifetime or ten. This violates nature's principle of holding no surplus, of gathering one's food—"capital"—on a daily basis, in the faith and trust that nature's beneficence will replenish tomorrow what is eaten today. The drive to accumulate surplus arises in a culture without spiritual life, when the urge toward self-fulfillment is perverted into the amassing of material goods as the sole standard of meaning.

Allowing unfettered accumulation leads to violation of another law of nature's economy, that of balance. Whereas nature brings extremes back toward the center, pure capitalism results in the opposite: a polarity of rich and poor, the rich owning the means of production and feeding off the labor of the poor. In this century, the moral outrage over such a system led to demands for governmental action to right the balance; most western economies are now a mix of free enterprise and government programs redistributing wealth and creating "balance," a middle class, softening the rough edges of the rich-poor polarity.

Because such governmental programs, however well-intentioned, do not address the fundamental source of the imbalance, they are ultimately ineffective in healing the economy; witness the rise of the homeless concurrent with the extraordinary wealth of those manipulating the economy with takeovers and junk bonds. If the root source of imbalance is not faced and resolved, the extremes become more extreme until the system collapses.

Finally, capitalism is fueled by the goal of perpetual growth. This fixation with linear economic growth violates nature's principle of working in cycles, feedback, loops. Since western culture's economy is built on the two pillars of consumerism and war, and since both pillars require the destruction of natural resources, the goal of perpetually expanding such an economy is ultimately suicidal. Like a feckless heir carelessly spending his inheritance, western culture grinds up its capital—natural resources—far faster than nature can replace it. The ultimate outcome of such a system is not only collapse of the economy, but of the global ecosystem as well.

While capitalism is in harmony with nature's fundamental urge toward self-fulfillment, the spiritual barrenness of western culture leads its capitalist economies to violate virtually every other natural law. As we have seen, such a system cannot be sustained indefinitely and must ultimately collapse.

The Principles of Communism

Communism arose as a protest against the horrific injustice of capitalism as practiced in the nineteenth century, the extreme poles of rich and poor, the atrocious working conditions and hours, the enslavement of children, the abject disregard for the human dignity of workers. Despite its noble intentions, in its formulation communism violates the one natural law capitalism embraces, that of allowing unfettered effort toward self-fulfillment, perverted as that may be into material accumulation. Rather than allowing each person the hope and opportunity to earn and keep the fruits of his labors, communism absorbs all effort into one centralized structure—the state—which takes it upon itself to distribute the nation's wealth as it deems proper.

In nature, animals are known to risk and sacrifice themselves for the sake of others within their herd. Parents will defend their young to the point of injury or death. The motives for such behavior are the same as those driving similar human acts: defense of loved ones and community. The willingness to engage in such acts is limited to a creature's immediate circle of family and herd; no creature considers the "greater good" of other species as motivation for its actions. Further, any act of risk or sacrifice is always voluntary, and the limits of sacrifice individually determined.

While communism may seem to be built upon nature's principle of balance, it violates the even deeper principle of freedom of self-fulfillment. Further, it achieves its balance through the forced participation of all workers sacrificing their labor for the "common good." Because sacrifice in nature is always voluntary and limited to one's immediate circle, communism's forced sacrifice violates natural law.

Nowhere is this more apparent than in the limited allowances of private property sometimes allowed in communist regimes. A privately owned plot of land is miraculously four times more productive than a state-owned plot next to it. Does privately owned soil carry more nutrients and receive favorable treatment from sun and rain? The difference lies in the consciousness of the farmer tending such plots; when his urge toward self-fulfillment is granted free play, he naturally works harder and with more care to produce a bountiful crop.

If capitalism and mainstream religion peacefully coexist, each minding its business without influence or interference from the other, communism takes a far more active interest in the spiritual life of its people: spirituality must be crushed. Unconsciously recognizing the profound spiritual violation communism represents, communist leaders know they must crush any outside loyalties or bonds which would lessen devotion to the state or restore spiritual truth to their people. That such a system profoundly violates natural law need hardly be stated; the spiritual emptiness of western culture reaches its nadir in the enforced atheism of the communist state.

As many have noted, communism seems so ideal in principle and always manifests so wretchedly in practice. Indeed, the ideal communist state—where everyone's needs are met and all work in harmony for the common good—is precisely how nature works. But because western culture is fundamentally divorced from nature, no structure built upon this violative foundation can operate in harmony with natural law. Communism, arising as a reaction against capitalism's violations, is itself an even greater violation. As a result, it is doomed to collapse sooner and with a greater crash than capitalism—as is being borne out in communism's continued decline.

The collapse of communism does not represent the triumph of capitalism. It means that communism was the greater violation, and that capitalism's day of reckoning lies still ahead.

The Natural Human Economy

If capitalism and communism, the two main economic structures of western culture, must ultimately fail, then what will replace them? How would an economic system in harmony with nature's principles be shaped?

Before we examine the details of such an economy, we must look to the very root of western culture's crisis: western culture has no genuine spiritual life. A spiritual system originating millennia ago in a distant time and place, now frozen into fossilized ritual and dogma, carries no vibrancy or power to speak to Space Age culture. It takes the threat of global extinction, of ecocide, to force modern culture to recognize fundamental truth: the human species holds no dominion over the earth but is inextricably interwoven with all other species in the web of life. The emerging holistic worldview, now coalescing at the cutting edge of cultural thought, represents a profound shift in consciousness, a recognition of the interdependence of all life, and carries within it the seeds of a new spirituality.

This spiritual revolution will heal western culture's most gaping wound: its existential insecurity in the face of a capricious creator, or of meaningless existence in an empty void. Once each person feels within himself the pulsing spiritual warmth infusing all creation, the need for external, material standards of self-worth will fade. Gone will be the frantic accumulation of wealth and property as the sole expression of the urge toward self-fulfillment. In its place will come a calm and inviolate security born of one's innate divinity and intrinsic worth in a universe suffused with meaning.

Building upon such a sturdy spiritual foundation, a healthy human economy will evolve in harmony with nature's principles. The most profound change will be in the approach to capital and private property. Capital—ownership of the means of production—and private property—purchased "rights" to control land—will undergo radical reformation.

The sharp demarcation between owners and workers which now marks capitalist economies will evolve toward greater worker participation and ownership. In harmony with nature's urge toward self-fulfillment, workers will enjoy the fruits of their labors in proportion to the overall health of the enterprise, rather than receiving a given wage regardless of profit. Already this trend is seen as workers demand "profit sharing" payments. As this trend continues, a more holistic approach to business will emerge in which workers and management view themselves as interconnected and mutually dependent parts of the whole, and therefore equally sharing in an enterprise's profit or loss. Another aspect of this trend is the rise of worker-owned businesses, where the owner class has been eliminated. These are the first steps toward the evolution of the ownership of capital.

More fundamental will be change in thinking about private property. Only a culture divorced from nature could devise a system in which one can purchase the rights to own and destroy the earth's skin with impunity. Ascending above "property rights" will be moral laws which dictate the use of land. The total acreage one person may own will shrink to what is reasonably required for one's home and garden; the rest will be common land for the benefit of all. Such a trend is evident in the land trust movement, where ownership of land is held by the community, and only dwellings are privately held. The right to alter land or build upon it will take into account the larger biotic community, as the impact of change on the greater ecosystem must be considered. Plants and animals will be understood to have rights to seek self-fulfillment in their natural homes, undisturbed by man; as of now, only endangered species are granted this respect, and only marginally.

Beneath these changes in the approach to private property will be the recognition that no one can own the earth; it is given freely, without deed or mortgage, to all species as a divine crucible for growth and exploration. Property rights will be subordinated under higher moral law. This understanding will naturally evolve in a culture restored to a genuine spiritual life.

All other principles of the natural economy will find expression in the human economy as well. The principle of balance means an end to extremes of wealth and poverty. The restoration of balance of wealth cannot be accomplished through force—a violation—but through each person's taking care of his reasonable needs, with perhaps a monetary equivalent of the squirrel's cache in the bank, and no more. Such an approach to personal wealth will evolve in step with the restoration of community as the basic unit of human culture, as those of working age contribute to sustaining the young and old, in the security of knowing their needs will be met should life's vicissitudes render them unable to care for themselves. While government is now the provider of such security, its future shrinkage will return the responsibility to its proper place, the community.

Finally, an economy in harmony with natural law will operate in recognition of nature's cyclicity rather than in pursuit of perpetual growth. Natural resources will be utilized only at the rate that nature can replace them. This means a simpler, less materialistic lifestyle. It means a reduction in the human population, as the current numbers far exceed the earth's capacity to sustain them. It means knowing the source of what one buys, that no violation has been committed in a product's creation. It means recycling every possible scrap. It means caring for one's body as the vehicle of consciousness, while recognizing that the only worthy life is one spent in growth and experience which elevates the spirit and endures beyond release of physical form.

Such an economic revolution is but one facet of the larger spiritual revolution now swelling beneath the crumbling foundations of western culture. No one will *impose* such a new economic order; it will arise naturally, organically, from a people restored to their natural and spiritual origins.

When each person feels the innate divinity pulsing within, senses the interconnection with all of life, and lives consciously in harmony with natural law, then all cultural expressions—politics, religion, economics—will naturally be transformed. Such is the new economic order, the New Age, toward which you are headed.

UFOs and Alien Visitors:
Invasion or Fantasy?

The "visitor" phenomenon is the latest version of a process which has accompanied the human species throughout its
history. The current manifestation stands unique, however,
because it is inextricably linked to the global crisis now looming before you. The phenomenon is in fact the result of several factors, which we shall explore one at a time.

First is the partnership between the human species and its
spiritual source. Communication between the spiritual realm
and the human species has guided your race from time imme-
morial; and in those early days, was consciously understood
and accepted as an essential and intrinsic part of the human
experience. In the millennia since, human cultures have constructed pantheons of gods, demons, angels, cherubs, and
fairies as symbols of the basic reality that you are never alone,
never cast adrift in an empty universe, but are forever cush-
ioned and guided by the spiritual realm.

Your earth is now at the most crucial danger point of its
history, for you hold in your power both the capacity to destroy yourselves with nuclear death and to make the planet
unlivable through environmental degradation. However large
the problems of the past, never has the planet as a whole faced
such dire peril, literally threatening to unravel nature's me-
ticulously interwoven web of life.

Flipping this situation over, examining the positive side, never have you held such opportunity to correct your course, to do so en masse as a unified people and race. For ecological catastrophe respects no boundaries; neither does radiation. You will face up to these problems as a species, united, or will perish in the detritus of your common ignorance. Because the times are so dire, the consequences so frightful, there is a deep unconscious cry sent out by your species to the spiritual realm, pleading for guidance. While there is always an unconscious flow between spiritual and human realms, in times of great peril the human species sends up shoots of urgency as it seeks to forge a new worldview and thus avert catastrophe.

In terms most difficult to explain, you share the physical space of your planet with many different "versions" of the planet's history. All time is simultaneous. All probable and parallel earths exist at the same time, in the same space. You are prevented from conscious awareness of other probable earths because each probable earth carries a distinct vibrational frequency at its core. Each individual also carries a unique vibrational frequency carried within the spine, which "locks" one into experiencing life on a particular probable earth. A soul seeking rebirth will search out the probable earth, the time period, the inherent challenges of the era and so forth, most in harmony with the soul's desired experience and growth. Once the selection of a probable earth is made, one aligns oneself with that earth not only by choosing parents who are already upon it, but by configuring one's intrinsic core energy to align with the axis of that probable earth.

Thus you share the physical space of your planet with an infinite variety of probable earths, while under ordinary circumstances never becoming aware of the other versions which occupy the same space. You are tuned to a very narrow band or frequency and all else is lost to you, just as many radio or television programs are broadcast simultaneously but you can tune into only one frequency, one program, at a time.

When a probable earth such as yours sends up a universal cry for guidance, in a sense you weaken, or make more permeable, the normally rigid barrier between probable earths. While you normally rest safe and sound in the illusory bed of your reality, times of peril and danger can weaken the membrane between probable earths as you seek to draw in alternate frequencies other than the one on which you and your planet operate.

There are probable earths on which the human species never deviated from living in harmony with nature's principles. There are probable earths reduced to radioactive cinder. As you stand at the brink of catastrophe, your need for information and guidance is so great that you weaken the normally impermeable barrier between probable earths to perceive how other civilizations have handled similar problems and challenges, and to learn from them quickly, rather than through trial and error as you normally would.

When the normally rigid barrier between probable realities is weakened, it is possible that those in other realities may take advantage of this in order to expand their field of knowledge, just as you seek to expand your field of knowledge by drawing upon the experiences of others. Just as you might be curious about the evolutionary progress on other realities radically different from your own, so it stands to reason that beings from other realities would find you of interest. This does not mean you are at their mercy. It means that if you make the choice, on unconscious levels, you may be open to visitation.

Everything you physically perceive is simply the result of electromagnetic waves being interpreted in highly specific and unique fashion by your senses. Your eyes see along a narrow band of vibration; your ears hear along another band of vibration. Other species do not interpret physical reality as you do; some have far broader ranges of perception, some can perceive what is invisible or silent to you. So all physically experienced phenomena are your unique interpretations of essentially nonphysical energy. You see one version of a given reality while others with different visual perceptive mechanisms would see something entirely different, and both would be equally valid. You are always *interpreting* when you experience the physical world, not perceiving a bedrock reality.

Given this, the visual and aural experiences of those receiving "visitors" will be their interpretation of essentially nonphysical material. Visitations are not intrusions of actual physical beings but psychological intrusions, interpreted by your senses as physical manifestations. The "beings" seen and heard are psychological projections from probable earths, oozing through the now-permeable barrier between probable realities.

Because you automatically assume, or your brain is conditioned to assume, that the highest form of life is man, you will automatically imbue such creatures with humanoid characteristics such as arms, legs, heads, etc. Yet the psychological structures involved are so radically and impossibly different from your own that the brain cannot fully mask them as human, cannot hallucinate these beings into appearing completely human. The brain goes as far as it can in interpreting these beings along the lines of its neuronal structures, but at some point this breaks down for these are indeed beings—psychological beings—so utterly foreign to your experience that the brain is unequipped to experience them in their true form. As in a dream, the brain squashes essentially nonphysical material down into symbol as a way of making it palatable, or understandable, to the everyday waking consciousness.

In deepest terms, the intruders are psychological beings who would best be interpreted as bodies of light, amorphous and vaporous. Yet your brain is not innately equipped to make this interpretation, for it senses also the great intelligence and curiosity of these beings. Unable to create the hallucination of an intelligent, curious cloud of vapor, the brain must struggle to render the image in more palatable, traditional terms. It does so by forcing a hallucination of as humanoid an appearance as possible, granting them limbs and eyes and so forth.

You see now why these beings don't leave evidence of windows and doors ajar, or other forced entry. They are not physical beings. They are psychological entities, interpreted by the brain within the limitations of its design.

The experiences some have of being transported, of finding themselves aboard space ships and so on, are psychological events interpreted in physical fashion. The visitors are interested in probing the human psyche, for it contains all knowledge of the condition, evolution and history of your planet. There is no need to rend the body asunder to find this information; it is all contained within the psyche, invisible to you. Again, any such experience of having one's psyche probed and examined will be interpreted in physical terms because there is no other way for the brain to render a satisfactory explanation to itself of what occurred. You cannot wake up and say, "I had my psyche probed last night." You do not know where your psyche is, if you acknowledge having one at all, and there is literally no way for your brain, as it has evolved in your framework, to absorb and express the event. It must be interpreted along the lines of its training and structure, rendering a psychological event as a physical event.

The body is a reflection of the psyche. It is the physical version of the psyche you carry with you from birth to death. If your psyche is probed in unfamiliar, uncomfortable ways, it stands to reason there may well be a physical aftereffect, for the body faithfully reflects the condition of the psyche. Scars, residual feelings of pain and so on, are pulsations from the psyche, expressions of the unfamiliar intrusion.

Let us broaden our discussion to some of the other physical effects beyond bodily effects: the sighting of lights in the sky, space ships, unusual lights and noises in the home, and so on.

There are essentially three levels of energy density on your level of awareness: thought, event and object. In basic terms, everything of which you are aware—from your briefest thought to the tallest mountain—is composed of grids of electromagnetic energy. The density of these grids determines whether they are experienced as thought, event or object.

As we have said, the experiences of those receiving "visitors" are psychological events, interpreted by the brain as physical events. As these psychological beings from probable realities approach your system, they must intertwine their unique energy with that of your planet, in a sense creating a hybrid energy, a bridge, across which they can travel. There will be blending, mixtures of energy and intent as the desire to cross the threshold intensifies. Again, human eyes may interpret these amorphous grids of energy and intent along physical lines: as lights, space ships and so forth.

Frequently an individual receiving "visitors" will become aware of such manifestations, whether as lights in the house or crafts in the sky, because that individual has agreed—on levels unconscious—to participate in the event. These sightings are the first indications or portents that a probable reality is oozing through the membrane into yours.

Those who have chosen to participate will find themselves aware of such phenomena precisely because they are precognitively aware of the impending visitation. Again, the brain struggles to make physical sense of a psychological phenomenon: energy crossing the normally impermeable boundary between probable realities.

Children, of course, are particularly susceptible to visitations and visual and aural manifestations because they reside always in the natural order—where such events are not feared but welcomed and intuitively understood. As the process of socialization and growing up in your culture is one of increasing divorce from the natural order, the adults involved may either blank all such memories out of consciousness or find them deeply frightening experiences. The line between dream and waking reality is far more permeable to the child than to the adult; so when the line between parallel realities becomes similarly blurred there is little cause for panic or even concern. It is accepted as a natural occurrence, as natural as the tide and rain. It is adults who encrust their experiences with fear, thus crippling their own recall and rendering the recalled events as fearful.

In very, very rare instances the thrust from a probable reality will be of such an intensity that there may be a residual physical mark left on the earth. This is extremely rare. For all the thousands of reports of sightings and visitations, you see why there is so little evidence—so little physical evidence—of the visitations. They are primarily psychological events.

Who are the psychological beings probing your reality? What is the nature of their civilization, and why are they poking about at this time?

Just as your culture and world cry out for guidance in this perilous time, so will others be motivated to seek information of assistance to their tottering civilizations. A content, stable, happy civilization would have no reason to cross the barrier between probable realities. It is only those in trouble to some degree who would take advantage and slip across the barrier.

As such, there may well be elements of desperation and arrogance on the part of those crossing over—for like your species plundering the natural and animal worlds desperately seeking cures for the diseases which are products of your culture, so can other civilizations conduct themselves with an urgency precluding tact and consideration. If they were not desperate for knowledge, they would not be here.

In a sense, the beings involved are highly evolved in technological and scientific terms while woefully lacking in an emotional component. The energy sent off by your species is one of great emotional turmoil because you have created weapons with which to destroy yourselves and find yourselves in the dilemma of not having the courage or wisdom to eliminate them. Your problems are not technological problems as much as they are human, emotional problems—how can we learn to love and trust one another? So it is this flavor to your crisis which attracts these beings, who find themselves bereft of an emotional component to their civilization and understand intuitively the importance of emotion without knowing precisely how to go about installing it among themselves.

So to plumb the depths and reaches of the human psyche, as they are doing, is a way of finding out what makes humans tick—and cry, and laugh, and love. You can see right away the intrinsic fallacy at work: how can one scientifically evaluate the importance of emotion and human kindness? All such is entirely outside the realm of science. Just as your sense mechanisms often distort reality, rendering psychological events as physical occurrences, so is their basic approach similarly askew, rendering them unable to obtain the knowledge they so ardently desire. You cannot rip apart a corpse, examine the heart, and determine the nature of love! And yet this is what this civilization, in its ignorance, is attempting to do.

Because your culture is scientifically backward compared to theirs, and because science is held as the pinnacle of a civilization's worth, it naturally follows that there may be a certain arrogance or disregard for your dignity on their part as they conduct their explorations. Do you not demonstrate similar contempt for every species other than your own, ripping them apart to understand what makes them tick, in order to alleviate your self-imposed suffering? The same process is at work in this instance of cross-barrier contact.

There is also a certain awe, though, a certain respect for the human species because it has this mysterious, magical quality of emotion which is incomprehensible to them, not reducible to equations and diagrams, and yet seemingly so rich, so wondrous. You view exotic native peoples of the globe in the same way: you envy their deep instinctive harmony with the earth, their fantastical rituals and beliefs, their rich and dark history; yet you are not ready to invite them home for dinner! The approach is the same here: one of interest and probing, but also a somewhat fearful hanging back lest one be overwhelmed by a foreign culture.

We affirm that you are at the mercy of nothing, and nothing may enter your life but that which you draw to yourself. In the individuals involved in visitations, there may be a sense of foreboding about the fate of the planet, about the future, or fear for one's children in a world so sick. It is precisely these individuals whose psyches cry out the loudest for guidance from beyond; thus they render themselves more open to visitation than those who hold no such fears and worries. The worries themselves weaken the barrier between realities and, on an individual level, contribute to the drawing in of "visitor" experience.

However frightening such experiences may be, nonetheless they serve to blast apart one's previously narrow view of reality, as inculcated from childhood, and that is precisely the point. Such individuals can never again walk through their days accepting scientific dogma without question; they know something very much deeper is out there. This is the first step for such individuals to begin a spiritual quest, if they choose to make it, for they can never go back to the old style of thinking, the traditional western worldview. Such a worldview has no place for "visitor" experiences, so unless one is willing to declare oneself insane, it is the traditional worldview that must be discarded.

In its place, if fears do not block the process, can be a blossoming of enlightenment and spiritual growth which can indeed help right the planet's course. Those individuals involved in "visitor" experiences feel the most anguish about the planet's condition, thus opening themselves to contact from alternate realities, and ultimately that experience forces fundamental shifts in their way of thinking. So the challenge is met, the cry is answered, the mind is expanded, the soul is nourished.

To sum up, the "visitor" experience is a blend of several conditions: your species crying out for spiritual guidance, weakening the membrane between probable realities; the brain's struggle to render unfamiliar psychological events in physical terms; and your species' rich emotional life serving as the focus for civilizations collapsing from excessive rationalism. As with every experience, those involved in "visitations" have made the choice, albeit unconsciously, to participate, and their experiences serve to trigger a spiritual search for meaning which may ultimately help heal your earth's malaise.

❖   ❖   ❖

When Alexander finished his delivery, I asked him to comment on a germane experience of mine. While driving cross-country I stopped for the night in a deserted little park in Nevada, rich with Indian petroglyphs. I spread my sleeping bag under the stars and drifted off to sleep.

I awoke to find myself bathed in a beam of white light of such intensity that my shadow on the ground was as crisp as beneath the noonday sun. The light's source hovered overhead, invisible and utterly silent. Naturally frightened by what I assumed was a top-secret military craft, I threw my gear in the car and rolled down the dirt road leading to the highway. The brilliant cold beam tracked the car until I pulled on the car's headlights. In a matter of seconds the light streaked across the broad sky and vanished. Relieved, I turned around, tossed my bag back on the ground, and fell asleep.

I awoke later to find myself again illuminated by the brilliant white light beaming from a stationary, silent source. This time I merely shrugged, rolled over, and went back to sleep.

This points out a subtle but striking aspect of the experience: some of my reactions and behavior seemed oddly cavalier and my thinking skewed. Certainly the military has developed closely guarded advanced technologies, but craft which hover in total silence and rocket across the sky without a sound are not now among them. Yet this was the conclusion—in retrospect, a preposterous one—I came to in convincing myself I need not be overly concerned. To merely shrug and roll over while under the scrutiny of an intense light in the sky seems inordinately blasé, as if my normal triggers of alarm and retreat had been deactivated.

Again, this was an event of psychological dimensions, interpreted as physical. You certainly saw the light and the shadow cast upon the ground. You have always been psychic, always open to the dimensions beyond the physical earth, and thus you were the natural candidate to be "scanned," as it were, by those easing across the membrane between realities. You were open to the experience, in other words, and thus drew the "light" of attention to yourself.

"I think it was a craft in the air shining a spotlight. I know what I saw."

In physical terms you are correct: it *was* a craft shining a spotlight. But, again, remember that everything of which you are physically aware is simply the physical version of a deeper event. In this case, the deeper event was perhaps even more awe-inspiring, if not fear-provoking: being "scanned" by the denizens of an alternate universe! Perhaps you would prefer just the spotlight! Again, because you are psychically open, you were being judged, in a way, as to whether you would be a suitable individual to participate in cross-barrier contact.

What dissuaded them was your independence—getting up and driving away, flashing them your headlights as a symbol of unintimidated aplomb, interpreted by them as defiance. This frightened them away, as you "saw" them speed across the night sky. Later they came back while you slept, intrigued by this fiery display of backbone, for such is unknown on their plane. They operate much more like robots. So while you were an object of some curiosity, you were rejected as a "subject" in their study due to your independence.

"Is it more than one parallel civilization responsible for all these contacts, or is it the same parallel earth?"

There are several civilizations involved. We say that knowing it to be a gross simplification, for it is difficult to honestly answer your question. You see, the closer civilizations are in terms of the core energy of their planets' axes and the energy fields of other parallel earths, the more likely contact is. In other words, virtually identical civilizations, while still riding on separate parallel earths, are able to make contact much more routinely than those on vastly different earths. The closer or more sympathetic are the vibrations, the easier the transmission between barriers.

So it is most accurate to say there is a cluster of similar civilizations who are crossing the barrier into your reality. These civilizations have communication among themselves, and play different roles in the process according to their abilities—which is why the "visitors" are often experienced as different shapes and forms; but more importantly, as different *volitionally*. Some pull the strings; some do the dirty work. The difference depends on which civilization they come from. There is enough sympathy among them that the cooperative joint venture can proceed to the benefit of all. From your perspective, these civilizations are all so radically different from yours, and yet so similar to each other, that they may essentially be thought of as one parallel reality—just as you have 50 states in an essentially unified country.

Supra-Consciousness: The Next Great Leap

While the Darwinian theory of evolution is creative fantasy, the human species does ride an evolutionary thrust. You were not cast upon the earth to stagger through successive ages of Bronze and Enlightenment and Space, somehow haphazardly weaving through the species' infinite potentials; you are guided and directed through time by an unfolding plan leading toward ever greater heights of spiritual and technological sophistication. Your species is not locked into forever experiencing the physical system through one slant of consciousness. Your consciousness is forever unfolding, expanding, accelerating.

To understand this process, and to understand whence you have come and where you are headed, we will examine the three main building blocks of human consciousness: the species' core vibration, the relationship between mind and matter, and the relationship between your waking self and authentic self. We will then be able to make better sense of the present time of social and spiritual upheaval, recognizing it as an essential step on the path toward future "supra-consciousness."

The Core Vibration

You know that the physical system is simply energy of various frequencies and patterns, coagulating into material structure. Consciousness, to operate within this system, must bind itself to matter, anchoring itself by decelerating its vibrational frequency to a degree compatible with matter. That is, consciousness bound to matter can operate only within a certain narrow band of frequency, slow enough to entrain with the frequency patterns underlying physical structure.

In any vertebrate organism, the spine carries a vibrational matrix of a frequency compromising between the frequencies of pure consciousness and the solidity of the material realm. This allows consciousness to flow through the organism's conscious mind, sending instructions to manipulate the earth, and then sending messages up from physical experience to the level of consciousness. This matrix of vibration encased in the spine we call the "core vibration."

The core vibration is more than simply the mediator between consciousness and matter. It will be set at birth to vibrate at a certain frequency, and this frequency—in the human species—determines the range of spiritual, intellectual, and technological experience available to the individual in that lifetime. If you think of ideas and experiences as bundles of energy—which they are—then the frequency of one's core vibration determines the upper and lower limits of the ideas and events one can experience. Again, consciousness can entrain only with matrices of energy of a roughly similar frequency, and all else outside this range will be invisible to the psyche.

You share your core vibration with all others of your generation. You all vibrate at the same basic frequency. This keeps human progress on a steady, even keel, for it keeps all members of a generation in the same basic range of spiritual and technical potential. While it may seem that there is an enormous difference between the far right and far left of your political spectrum and in the religious realm, in fact the range is relatively narrow, and is determined by the core vibration pulsing beneath your generation's experience.

Human "evolution"—which occurs in the realm of consciousness—is guided by a gradual acceleration of the species' core vibration. Each generation vibrates at a slightly higher frequency, allowing it to reach higher into the heavens and pull down ideas, inventions, and spirituality of greater sophistication, elegance, and truth than preceding generations could realize.

Within the range of potential undergirding each generation, most will fall at the midpoint, the center of the vibrational range, comprising the mainstream of society. These individuals are neither reactionary nor visionary, content to follow the customs of the day, never stepping too far outside the accepted ideas and trends. This great bulk of humanity acts to "digest" the visions of the prophets of spirit and technology, gradually pulling cutting-edge thought into everyday life. The psychologically rigid cling to the ideas of yesterday in reactionary fear, even as the mainstream has outgrown and discarded them.

You can visualize this process as a time line stretching from past to future; strung out along the time line are ideas and concepts, pulsating as bundles of potential. As the core vibration of the species accelerates, the range of human potential—see it as a band a few inches wide—moves further along the track, and cutting-edge thinkers will just be able to absorb fragments of those concepts lying at the upper end of the range. Over time, as the core vibration continually accelerates, each concept will move from cutting-edge to mainstream, then finally to reactionary, after which it will be dropped entirely from society's range of thought.

Another metaphor would be to see visionaries as the teeth of the species, biting off fragments of future potential; the mainstream as the digestive organs, breaking concepts down into practical terms and making them available to the larger body; and we leave it to the scatalogically minded to complete the metaphor vis-à-vis the function of the reactionary.

Let us look at an example. For centuries it was taken for granted as irrefutable truth that the black race was inherently inferior to the white, and that it was morally acceptable to buy and sell this inferior race as slaves. At some point, this began to grate on the conscience of a few individuals, dancing on the cutting edge of spiritual progress. When the abolitionist movement was born, its core idea—that blacks should be as free as whites—was so far ahead of the mainstream that its founders were branded lunatics.

Gradually, though, over generations, as the core vibration of the species accelerated and each new life brought a higher vibration to the species, more and more consciences were pricked at the immorality of slavery. The practice grated against the accelerating spiritual life of the species. As always, the dynamic play between visionary and reactionary played out, here in as brutal and graphic terms as the Civil War.

Now, consider the views on race of the most reactionary, bigoted fanatics in your day. The worst, most backward idea they espouse is that blacks should either be given a state of their own or that they be shipped back to Africa—the idea being that the races should be separate and blacks relegated to their own societies.

Three hundred years ago, this would have been visionary. The idea that blacks should be free to operate their own society, either within a set-aside portion of your country or returned to their African roots, would have been branded outrageous foolishness, being so far ahead of its time. Then, as the core vibration accelerated, and with slavery abolished, this idea held the mainstream—blacks may be free, but it would be better if they lived separately from whites; and so the era of segregation was born. And now, as the core vibration has accelerated still further and the spiritual midpoint is bumped still higher, the notion of segregating blacks into their own enclaves becomes anathema to the mainstream and is picked up by reactionaries clinging to the battered conceptual relics of the past.

So the same idea—blacks should be free to live within defined enclaves—has progressed over time from visionary to mainstream to reactionary. So it is with every idea, every religious system, every technology. As your core vibration accelerates, you reach ever higher potentials of spiritual, social, and technological growth.

The Mind Soars, The Body Crawls

Each cell of your body is conscious, has consciousness, is alert and alive. Because every cell knows that it participates in the larger and more complex structure of the body, it tunes itself to receive the richest, fullest stream of vibrational information. It does so by entraining itself to its two primary sources of such information: your core vibration and the belief filter through which your conscious mind processes experience.

It is automatic for a bodily cell to harmonize its vibrational frequency with the core vibration, for the steady pulsation emanating from the spine and nervous system sets the rhythm of the body, binding every cell in a shared cadence. This ensures that the body's organismic functions operate as smoothly and harmoniously as possible.

Yet each bodily cell also entrains itself to your conscious mind, for the body depends on the mind to apprise it of its stance in time and space, of conditions in the immediate environment, of potentials for danger and pleasure, and so on. In every moment of waking awareness you filter experience through your beliefs and values; you process raw sensory data through a "belief filter" which interprets that data.

This belief filter is a network of neuronal connections built up over your lifetime, literally etching into the brain your beliefs about yourself, others, the world at large. The belief filter has an electromagnetic reality, for it is the portal through which sensory data vibration is translated into thought vibration. Because the body's cells strive to receive as clear a picture as possible of where you are and what is happening around you, they entrain their vibrational patterns with your belief filter. In this way, your beliefs are literally etched into every cell of your body.

The greatest harmony between mind and body is forged when the ideas in the belief filter are of the same general vibrational level as the core vibration pulsing through the cells—when the two sources of vibrational information for the body entrain in smooth harmony, creating a powerful, unified gestalt of mind and matter. So much of your language betrays this understanding: you say you believe something "with every fiber of my being." When an idea grates against your beliefs you say, "It does not resonate with me." Your language illumines your understanding that highest harmony is reached when mind and body operate "on the same wavelength."

Thus the mainstream is the most comfortable place to be, for mind and body are firmly rooted at the midpoint of a generation's range and communicate with highest clarity. Visionaries and reactionaries, in contrast, lose the harmony between mind and body. Their ideas—lofty or primitive—push at the extreme edges of the range of potential and the body cannot follow, cannot accelerate or decelerate its core vibration to match the belief filter. The smooth harmony between mind and body is impaired because the body's range of potential is much narrower than the far reaches of consciousness.

You know how often genius is equated with madness, emotional and personal turmoil, the inability to fit in with society. Here, the mind leapfrogs into future potentials but the body cannot follow; this schism creates disharmony between mind and body manifesting as a turbulent, unstable psyche—the blessing and curse of genius.

Mind and Matter: A Rocky Relationship

Whether you consider that thoughts are things and objects are things, or that thoughts are vibration and objects are vibration, you drive toward the same truth: the material world is composed of the same basic "stuff" as your consciousness. It's all a pulsing vibrational swirl, some of it denser and slower than the rest, and this you perceive as physical matter.

What is the relationship between mind and matter? First, understand that the core vibration of your species is in turn regulated by the core vibration of the planet, what we might call the "planet pulse." This planet pulse serves as the unifying tone of the earth system, binding all plants and animals in a shared framework in which matter has a consistent density and the ability of consciousness to manipulate matter is constant across all species.

The slower the vibrational pattern behind a body of matter, the more the laws of electromagnetism govern, especially the "gravity" between cells of matter. The impulse of a material cell is to bind with others of like construction and thus to create structures enduring through space and time. The slower the vibrational pattern, the stronger the gravitational bonds between cells will be and the more impervious to manipulation by organisms animated by consciousness, or by pure consciousness.

Thus, as the planet pulse gradually accelerates over time, thereby accelerating the fields of vibration manifesting as matter, they become less dense, less solid, and more amenable to manipulation. The gravitational bonds weaken, allowing consciousness to seep into the vibrational pattern, thus enhancing your power of manipulation. Because you know only your time and place, it may be difficult to imagine that the objects of the physical world once weighed more than they do now for a given volume, or that rocks and water are somehow lighter than they have been in the past. Yet this is the case.

You are intrigued by magicians' tricks in which objects seem to float through the air under direction of the magician's mind, or by the possibility of levitation and spoon bending. These reflect your unconscious knowing that the relationship between mind and matter is malleable, not etched in stone (so to speak), and that as time rolls forward matter becomes less dense and thus more receptive to your manipulation. The magic tricks compel you so because they offer hints of future potential.

Waking Self/Authentic Self

The third primary structural component of human consciousness is the relationship between the conscious mind or "waking self" and your "authentic self," that vast pool of consciousness in whose deep waters you swim in the dream state every night. There must be a barrier, a wall, between these two selves, for your conscious mind must first concern itself with maintaining your security and translating thought into action—it cannot simultaneously converse with your reincarnational selves and bake a cake.

Still, the permeability of the wall between waking and authentic selves is greatly influenced by your beliefs about the authentic self and its value to you. If you were raised to believe that you are inherently evil, you will suppress and deny all messages from your authentic self, and the wall will grow hard and rigid. If you cherish your impulses and dreams, frequently falling asleep while surrendering problems to resolution in the dream state, you open the wall to being far more elastic and permeable.

Your authentic self is your true self, for it directly communicates with your higher self and your reincarnational and probable selves, detects future events approaching manifestation, maintains contact with those you care about in the dream state, and so on. All of this information can be available to your waking mind *in symbolic form.*

That is, the authentic self cannot simply dump its messages into your conscious mind in their full vibrant totality; your conscious mind could not endure the sudden acceleration. Such messages must be decelerated to harmonize with your conscious mind, and in doing so they lose some fidelity and richness, leaving you with symbols, fragments, impulses— much as the symbology of dreams is the patina painted by the conscious mind over deeper nonphysical experience.

Just as the body rides the planet pulse, so is the permeability of the wall between waking and authentic selves regulated to some extent by both your core vibration and belief filter. That is, no matter how expansive your beliefs, or how much you welcome a flood of information from your authentic self, your core vibration acts as a screen demarking the limits of what information can be transmitted.

It isn't intended that the barrier become floodgates, allowing unhindered flow from your deeper self into your waking mind. You are physical creatures designed to operate in a physical system, and as such your waking focus must always be on physical safety and manipulation of the earth. At best, your authentic self impinges on waking consciousness through clear impulses to action which are honored, respected, and followed through.

It should be apparent that the three structural components of human consciousness are not immutably prewired into the species, but change over time as the core vibrations of the species and planet accelerate. Each generation reaches higher into spiritual and technological potential; matter and the body's cells become less dense and more receptive to consciousness; and the barrier between waking and authentic selves becomes more permeable because an accelerated waking consciousness can handle a greater flow of impulse from the authentic self, "stepping down" fewer levels of deceleration and thereby retaining greater fidelity. So the grand human experiment is set up to unfold over time as a gradual expansion of your spiritual and scientific life; to offer greater mastery and manipulation of the earth; and to expand the flow between waking self and authentic self.

You may look back in history and scoff at your barbarian forebears, burning each other at the stake as homage to the Church, but recognize that the core vibration of the species was vastly slower then, meaning the culture was bound to a primitive spiritual potential and the barrier between authentic and waking selves was as a steel wall. Recognize also that someday your era's highest spiritual potential will cause bemused heads to shake at the primitivism of the late twentieth century.

Spiritual Growth: To Crawl Or To Leapfrog?

As a general rule, the species flows evenly along the linear time line, gradually accelerating its core vibration and reaching higher into its potentials. Each generation offers the height of its achievement as teaching to the next, which in turn builds upon that foundation to attain even greater sophistication of its spiritual and technical models.

There are times when the process of accelerating the species' core vibration is not so much a crawl as a leapfrog: a sudden acceleration of the species' core vibration catapults society into chaos as the old institutional foundation crumbles and a new framework has not yet been assembled. These are times of great upheaval and chaos, when fanaticism and reactionary hysteria rise even as others struggle to forge a richer cosmology as the foundation of society.

There are times when this acceleration, while sudden and sharp, nonetheless represents a refining of an old worldview and not its complete abandonment. During the last intersection of the Christ Entity with your plane, Jesus offered a revision of the Old Testament image of Jehovah as a fierce, jealous and murderous deity; Jesus offered a God of love and forgiveness, and taught that the healthiest society was based on mutual love and respect among neighbors. This was a laughable prospect to a culture seething with ancient animosities and perpetual vendettas—as plays out still in the Middle East—but nonetheless Jesus refined the extant image of God rather than jettisoning Him entirely.

You Create Your Own Reality—Sometimes

Two thousand years later, you stand at the cusp of another sudden acceleration, yet the difference is that you are not refining western culture's traditional worldview, you are abandoning it. The transition from a world in which God, fate, or dumb luck rules your lives to one in which each individual creates his or her own reality is not a crawl but a leapfrog—a leapfrog over a very deep chasm. There is no smooth transition between the two worldviews; the old must be jettisoned for the new to take root.

If the core vibration of the species is accelerating, meaning the midpoint of society is rapidly shooting toward this new understanding, then those clinging to old thinking unconsciously feel the energy being cut out from under them. Born into the mainstream, they now feel themselves increasingly alienated and abandoned—thus the hysteria among the far right wing in its religious, political, and anti-abortion expressions.

At the same time, the mainstream feels threatened as the ground shifts beneath its feet and it loses its sturdy foundation. Traditional institutions—education, health care, politics, even the family—all seem to be crumbling; and political attempts to patch them together with money and regulation are futile.

You are on the brink of a sudden acceleration into a new way of thinking and being, and it requires a leap of faith—literally—over the chasm between the old worldview and the new. The challenge is that, while your minds may welcome the change and struggle to usher in the vaunted New Age, your bodies cannot entirely follow.

Remember that the core vibration is implanted at birth and remains constant, thus demarking the limits of cellular consciousness. The mind is far more elastic, being pure consciousness, and can leap forward to grasp hold of visionary ideas though the body cannot follow. The difficulties many of you experience in truly making real the concept that you create your own reality is that while your minds may believe it, your bodies cannot yet fully operate at that level of awareness.

Consider how long it will be before "you create your reality" is the fundamental operating principle of your society—two generations? three? At that point, the concept will be mainstream, meaning the species' core vibration will have aligned precisely with the idea. Mind and body will be harmonized to conduct daily life with "reality creation" as their basic operating principle; the body's cells, vibrating at a faster pitch, will be more receptive to consciousness, making healing of disease states more a process of inner work than external manipulation; and waking and authentic selves will exchange information in an open, rich dialogue.

Those of you who believe that you create your reality and have tried to put the concept into practice in your everyday lives may have felt frustrated at its apparent ineffectiveness. It does not work all the time, nor as quickly as you would like, nor with equal ease in every aspect of your life. We do not address an audience of overnight millionaires with life expectancies of 150 years, so there must be a gap between belief in creating one's reality and actually manifesting it.

That gap is the chasm between old order and new, which your mind can soar across to drink of the rich potential of the species while your body remains anchored to your present. Your minds push at the limits of their conceptual reach, but in so doing they lose full harmony with the body. Even if you renovate your belief filter to pulsate with pure clarity of this vision, your body's cells cannot match your mind's growth, cannot break free of the core vibration binding them to the mainstream worldview extant at your birth.

You see, it is for future generations, your children and grandchildren, to fully put into everyday practice the understanding that they create their reality. As the transitional generation, your role is to stretch your minds to absorb this new conceptual framework, put it into practice to whatever extent is possible within your life, and to pass this understanding on to your children. They know—they *know*—the truth of "reality creation" and won't share the struggle you undergo in attempting to make it work. It will work for them—like magic.

The next great leap of human evolution, then, is "supra-consciousness"—consciousness anchored to human form but with "reality creation" as its practical operating principle; a relationship between mind and matter inconceivable to you now (spoon bending will be mastered in kindergarten); and the ability to swim in the realms of the authentic self while conscious. All this on your continuing evolution into "bodies of light"—but that is another chapter.

Building Cities of Light

Human consciousness has always been present in the earth system. This is not to say that it has crystallized into human *form* in all historical periods. Because all time is simultaneous, earth and humanity are linked in the common experience of physical life, though the human species dips in and out of manifestation along the historical time line.

The earth has not always been as sturdy and permanent as you now know it. As earth consciousness first began to trickle into materialization, it manifested as patterns of light, of highly accelerated vibratory energy, as if playing with the notion of light and shadow before condensing further. As earth's energy patterns gradually solidified, the earth system became denser, more liquid than light, a fluid medium through which consciousness could begin to play with physical laws but in a gelatinous medium offering great ease of mobility and instantaneous transmission of thought.

The more the earth patterns solidified, the more they became governed by the laws of electromagnetism, especially gravity. Gravity is the tendency of material bodies to attract to each other, "magnetically" expressing their desire to form structures enduring through space and time. The stronger the magnetic bonds binding a material substance, the less receptive it is to influence or manipulation by consciousness. That is, consciousness can "seep" into the energetic fields lying behind a body of matter only to the extent those fields are open and permeable enough to allow it.

Over time, as the basic pulse of the planet accelerates, matter becomes lighter, meaning the vibratory patterns behind matter contain less "bulk," are less governed by the strong gravitational pull, and are therefore more receptive to manipulation by consciousness. Thus the relationship between mind and matter varies over time, and reflects whether the planet pulse is accelerating to allow easier manipulation or decelerating to close down the animate species' ability to manipulate matter.

This rhythmic process of gradually accelerating and decelerating the core vibration of the planet plays out over eons like a primal tide, ebbing and rising, and determines which species manifest in various historical periods. Because the relationship between consciousness and matter rhythmically flows with the primal tide, species will manifest when the right "mix" is present, when the optimal mind/matter relationship is present given a species' structure and desired experience.

A species manifests when the core vibration of the planet is in harmony with the species' bodily construction and supports the species' range of consciousness. The dinosaurs manifested in a period when the planet pulse was much slower than it is today, meaning that matter was denser and the gravitational pull between cells much stronger, allowing enormous bodies to manipulate effectively because their flesh was so dense, their bodies therefore so sturdy, and "held" to the earth with a magnetic pull difficult for you to conceive. If you think how awkward a dinosaur would be on the moon, where a slight movement might topple such a beast because it is not as "rooted" as it would be on earth, you catch a glimpse of how the relationship between the earth's pulse and the size of species upon it varies over time.

In addition, because consciousness is anchored to matter in the physical system, the vibrational frequencies of the earth determine which species can manifest in a given period. The dinosaurs, again, were animated by a consciousness playing out the predator-prey dynamic, meaning a step up from unicellular consciousness and requiring some awareness of relationships—if only the relationship with one's intended dinner. Still, this is a step "up" in consciousness from fungi and bacteria.

Human consciousness, a highly unique and highly accelerated brand of consciousness, requires a relatively accelerated planet pulse before it can manifest. As the species of symbolic manipulation—artists, craftsmen, builders, destroyers—the relationship between mind and matter must be relatively smooth and open, allowing you free rein to forge symbolic fragments of your consciousness in tools and art. Your bodies are large enough to allow effective mastery of the natural world, but not so large that they become unwieldy or force you to spend your waking hours foraging for food. They are lean and compact, requiring a minimum of energy to sustain your activities.

Because the planet pulse rises and falls, and human consciousness can manifest only within a certain band of planetary frequency, there are civilizations which gradually "decelerate" into primitivism and civilizations which gradually "accelerate" into spiritual and technological sophistication. Thus there are civilizations in your distant "past" which reached heights of achievement your culture can barely conceive of—for yours is an accelerating society with far to go before reaching the apex of its growth. These ancient civilizations serve as beacons of human potential; their achievements shimmer in the racial memory as icons of the species' highest promise, pulling you forward as you climb the accelerating planet pulse into building an ever more sophisticated culture.

Given that an accelerated planetary pulse weakens the gravitational pull between cells of matter, a civilization at the very apex of acceleration is best understood as a "city of light"—for many of the parameters of the physical system you take for granted are cast off; density melts to fluid, then light; thought no longer need be stepped down to symbolic speech, but is transmitted instantaneously as pure thought-form. Far fewer cells make up the human body and those cells are instantly receptive to communication from the mind.

Your images of ancient civilizations are often of brilliantly white cities shimmering with effervescent light. This reflects your unconscious knowledge that these civilizations operated on the active principles of light and thought rather than matter and symbol, as you now do. Light and sound became the primary "tools" of these cultures. To offer several examples of how such a culture operates:

Once the human body is understood as a grid of vibrational energy of differing frequencies and patterns, a skilled healer can detect the location and severity of imbalance by singing to the body—literally sending out vibrational tones and determining the extent of resonance with the patient's body. A healthy body entrains with the vibrational fields around it; thus a healthy area of the body "sings back" to the healer. Where the body's song is weak or nonexistent, the healer knows a blockage is depressing the vitality of that area. Healing becomes a matter of stimulating the body with the depressed frequency until gradually the weakened area entrains with that frequency.

Skilled "song healers" work in pairs or larger groups, creating harmonies with their songs that match the harmonic patterns of the body. As many as a dozen song healers seat themselves in a circle around the afflicted one, building a rich resonance of harmonious tones which entrain the body and restore it to full vitality.

Energy production is also handled through sound. Certain light metals—not yet available to you because of the relative density of matter in your time—can be fashioned into exquisitely sensitive receptors of sound vibration, and can magnify that vibration such that the outflow of current exceeds the energy imparted to stimulate the machine. Large systems—for powering cities and cultural centers—contain built-in feedback loops so they perpetually stimulate themselves to produce current while siphoning the excess to productive use. Homes have smaller models tuned to human vocal frequencies, so one "sings for one's supper"—the supper in this case being the energy supply for the household.

Light is also a tool of healing. Pure sunlight, filtered through colored glass, prism, or crystal, depending on the application, is to medicine what the scalpel is to you today. Because light carries a much faster and more powerful vibrational field than either the human body or sound energy, it must be used sparingly and skillfully by those trained in its precise application. Where damage to the body is great and the trauma too severe to be healed through sound, light medicine offers a powerful, sudden acceleration of the afflicted area. Your crude tool of shock therapy is the first step in recognizing the power of a sudden "blast" of accelerated energy to the body.

Light medicine also offers a means to "burn out" a diseased or atrophied part of the body, if damage is too severe for healing to occur. This replaces surgical removal of body parts as is custom in your day, with its attendant severe trauma visited on the body.

Light medicine is the practice of the elite, a skilled coterie of healers who have mastered song healing and have developed their consciousness to the degree that they can mentally entrain with the consciousness of the patient's body and communicate with it telepathically to determine the location and extent of injury. This is essential since an individual suffering great trauma, as in your day, is frequently in shock or unconscious and unable to communicate. By bypassing the patient's intellect and conversing directly with his body, second-guessing and exploratory surgery are eliminated; the body participates in and largely directs its own healing.

Even smaller than the elite circle of light healers are the "moon healers," an exclusively female society of healers using moonlight as their energy source, again magnifying it through glass or crystal. Their emphasis is not so much on healing major trauma as on building a sororal order rich in ritual, mystery, and magic. Because the moon is bedrock and its reflected light is much softer than the sun's, moon healers develop skills far more subtle and gentle than the light healers funneling the sun's cacophonous vibrational stream—although most moon healers are light healers by day.

Because the moon is their guiding deity and the society exclusively female, its intent and purpose revolve around female experience: menstruation—binding moon and body in a common cycle—childbirth, midwifery, and so on. Most children born in these evolved civilizations do so under the care of moon healers, who communicate telepathically with the child in the womb and use their magnifying tools to invigorate the mother's or child's body should the need develop. Childbirth itself is a virtually painless experience as the mother, with the moon healers' aid, can mentally anesthetize her pelvic area, and the body's greater elasticity eases the child's expulsion from the womb.

Moon healers also call upon a profound body of knowledge concerning plants and herbs. This body of knowledge is passed on as part of the apprenticeship process, but the greatest source of such knowledge lies with the plants themselves. Of the profusion of plant life present in any era, a few will be designated as "teachers"; these, upon being ingested, link their consciousness with their human host and communicate telepathically. Questions about which healing plants to use, in what proportion, will be offered by the plant teachers. (Incidentally, you have plant teachers among you now, of course, but their use is a federal offense—a measure of the relative primitivism of your culture.)

You know you are on the "upswing" toward building an accelerated civilization because you have the first hints and fragments of this higher consciousness with you now. Books on using sound and light as tools of healing have begun to appear, the first fragments of a new foundation underlying your medical system. In time, over centuries, your culture will evolve to embrace an ever more sophisticated and spiritually pure consciousness, leading to the day when, like Atlantis and Lemuria and untold civilizations whose names are lost to time, you have built a new "city of light."

Between Parent and Child:
The Sacred Bond

Like prying open a crypt and throwing fresh light on hidden, moldering relics from the past, your society is finally unearthing its deepest, darkest secret: most family life sears its children with deep, lasting psychic scars, crippling emotional maturity and poisoning all of adult life with the toxic residue of parental abuse and neglect. In adulthood, these damaged children will in turn scar their children, another link in the chain of human tragedy uncoiling through the ages.

How to break free? How to overcome a toxic childhood and raise one's own children with their security, creativity, wonder, and spiritual vitality intact? Let us look first at the source of this chain of human misery.

The Sinner and the Atheist

Western culture offers not one but two cosmological perspectives on the origin of life. In one camp, the Judeo-Christian, the universe was created by God, an occasionally wrathful, occasionally benevolent creator who lives apart from His creation. In the Christian tradition, one is born in sin—carrying the sin-drenched legacy of the first human couple—and only through accepting Christ as one's personal savior can one find release from the inevitable descent to hell which is the fate of the unbaptized.

In the scientific camp, the universe is a meaningless accident, a result of uncountable chance events randomly coagulating into life inexplicably endowed with consciousness. Life's only purpose is to conquer one's competitors and produce as many offspring as conceivable, suffusing the species' gene pool with your chromosomal heritage.

These, then, are the two arbiters and definers of the meaning of life. Either you are born in sin, compelled to toe the straight-and-narrow line prescribed by religious authorities; or you exist on a planet without meaning, squiggling through your few paltry decades and then decaying into the void.

Whatever their surface differences, science and religion agree on certain fundamentals: you must not look inside yourself for life's meaning; you must not think of yourself as inherently divine; you must not rest secure in the knowledge that your consciousness is eternal and indestructible; you must not look upon yourself as a unique and irreplaceable contribution to the sweep of human and global history.

Western culture is founded on existential insecurity. You don't know who you are. You don't know why you are here. You don't know the underlying meaning of life. You don't understand the role you are to play in the drama. You don't feel your divinity pulsing in every vein. You don't recognize your kinship with the natural world. You are cut off, atomized, alone.

If this existential insecurity is the deepest core idea upon which the psyche is built, flavoring life's every moment and thought, then one is never truly secure. The most basic questions have not been answered. Like a noxious haze, this insecurity blankets even the most sublime moments of love, connection, and inspiration. Even the sacred bond between parent and child is sullied if the parent does not feel the divinity pulsing within himself and recognize it in the child's wondering, curious, loving eyes.

The Parent as Economic Fodder

It is beyond the scope of this essay to fully probe the process through which a curious, creative child willingly becomes the adult slave to work he does not enjoy, surrendering his personal fulfillment to responsibilities he never truly chose, but the most significant tool to this end is the suppression and demonization of impulses.

Impulses are the driving force of human progress, the probing, exploring, creative sparks of inspiration through which the child gains mastery of the world's structure and processes, and simultaneously impresses upon the world his unique, individual stamp of personality. The child seeks both to understand how the world works—and every culture, from the most primitive to the most technologically advanced, has its version of this knowledge—and to leave his private mark, his unique contribution to that world. In a dynamic process, he uses the extant structures and systems given him by his elders to build original and creative variations atop those systems.

Of course, this holds true in adulthood as well. Artists and technological innovators employ the same process—steeping themselves in the traditions of their fields, the better to grow beyond them and offer something new, better, improved, often arriving unbidden in sudden bursts of inspiration.

Perhaps the most pernicious legacy of the Judeo-Christian heritage is its demonization of impulses. If we are essentially sinful creatures, then all our impulses must be urges toward sin, and therefore must be suppressed. While the religious tradition has lost much of its power, its legacy of sin-stained impulse remains deeply embedded in the western psyche.

Observe parents and children and notice how many curious hands are slapped, how many innocent explorations meet with a furious "No!", how the impulse for movement is restrained. Multiply each day's several dozen such suppressions by the thousands of childhood days and the result is an adult willingly suppressing his own impulses, assuming the role of the slapping parental hand, the biting "No!", the directive to sit still and be quiet.

All societal structures participate in the suppression of impulse. The western educational system is perhaps the most obvious example: row upon row of neatly aligned desks, all eyes facing toward the teacher who disseminates while the children absorb, needing permission to speak, stand up, or use the bathroom. This grotesque perversion of children's natural urge to learn and explore sanctifies the parental injunctions awaiting the child upon return from school. If the child receives religious training in Sunday School, here again the child's innate, impulsive, divine nature is suppressed while millennia-old scriptures are laboriously memorized.

All societal structures join in the suppression and demonization of impulse because, above all, impulse suppression is essential to smooth functioning of the economy. Most people, given a choice, would not choose to do the work they do, to surrender their personal growth, fulfillment, and creative expression in order to make ends meet. A society of truly free, impulsively creative individuals brimming with zest for life would never tolerate the supremacy of economic considerations over all human, moral, and spiritual values. Whether communist or capitalist, western societies require a force of dependable, submissive, order-taking workers in order to maintain the economic machinery. It is to this end that parents, schools, and churches suppress free thought, curiosity, living for the present, pursuit of pleasure, and all other nefarious results of allowing impulses free rein.

You may protest that it is impossible to be a free spirit blithely floating through life without a care; one must either pay rent or a mortgage; one must feed oneself and not become a burden on others; one must plan for one's security in old age. These are all valid concerns, but only within the context of the present social system. The "rent or mortgage" dilemma arises from the western concept of private land owner-ship, an inconceivable notion to native stewards who once trod your land untroubled by housing affordability. So, yes, economic concerns are valid as long as the present system endures, but a change in consciousness will bring about a changed social and economic order with material concerns dropping below supreme spiritual and moral values.

This ties in with our discussion of parenthood because any individual, parent or not, who does work he does not enjoy because he feels he must to survive, is actively suppress-ing impulses toward personal growth and fulfillment in favor of economic security. The psyche plays host to a crippling dynamic where every impulse is scrutinized on the sole basis of its affordability. The urge to explore new places is chan-neled into brief and properly scheduled vacations. The urge to stand up for oneself and protest mistreatment is often squelched entirely out of fear of losing one's job. The urge to run out and play on a beautiful day is either suppressed or becomes a guilt-soaked "sick day." The urge to make love is granted expression only at the end of a long and tiring day, with the kids asleep.

The human cost of suppressing natural impulses and sur-rendering to the economic imperative is staggering beyond measure. It leads to alcohol and drug abuse. It leads to broken spirits, broken homes, broken lives. It leads to lives of quiet desperation. It leads to painful deathbed regrets. Most dam-aging of all, it leads to emotional, physical, and sexual abuse of children, who in their dependence and natural trust can only accept the abuse as their rightful due.

Children as Sex Objects

One of the darkest secrets to come out of breaking the long-standing taboo over honest examination of family pa-thology is the extent to which children are used for sexual gratification by family members. Molestation by strangers has always been a sad feature of western culture, but the emphasis now on abuse by parents and relatives forces an awareness of an issue long swept under the rug.

Most fundamentally, the driving force behind the sexual urge is not the urge for orgasmic release, but for *incorporation.* Exchange of energy at the auric level always occurs when another is within six feet of you, and the fidelity of transmission increases as the distance narrows. In sex, not only is the partner directly against you, skin to skin, but the nature of the encounter—a surrender to all-consuming passion and pleasure released from reason's grip—offers the deepest, purest exchange two bodies can know.

Since sexual desire is directed toward those who carry qualities and energies you lack and therefore desire to incorporate, the urge for sex with children arises in individuals who long for a return to childhood innocence, freed from the unbearable burdens and disappointments of adulthood. Unhappy men with jobs they hate, strangers to their wives or single, may turn to children as a symbolic means of returning to childhood, incorporating the energy of young souls unable to threaten adult rejection, unable to judge failings and lacks, unable to criticize, demean, scorn.

That sexual abuse of children is so widespread indicates the profound damage inflicted on the psyche, especially the male psyche, by your culture's worship of economic values above moral and spiritual values, by the imperative—especially for men—to suppress all impulse, never show emotion or cry, be a team player, and subjugate the self to economic security. For many such men, the only escape from an adult world offering crippling wounds to the psyche is to "incorporate" the energy of childhood—even if the means are so brutal a violation of a child's innocence and trust.

Spiritual Family Planning

To fully appreciate the bonds between parent and child, we must look beyond the traditional notion that the bond begins with the child's birth. A family constellation, in truth, is woven together long before the birth of children or even parents. Since the purpose of human life is to grow through challenges, a family constellation will be chosen to provide the psychic and psychological background most conducive to a soul's chosen growth. Karmic factors may also come into play, where two souls having built a relationship in another lifetime recast their joint challenge into the parent-child bond.

In choosing a family, the most significant factor considered is the spiritual state of the mother. By "spiritual" we do not mean her denomination or devotion to church attendance, but the vibrational caliber of her psyche. Each of you emanates a stream of vibrational energy of a "higher" or "lower" quality, serving both as a magnet to people and events of similar vibration, and delimiting the upper and lower boundaries of potential experience.

A woman carrying mainstream energy, of a vibrational pattern well within the norm for a given culture, will end up neither saint nor depraved, offering a bedrock cocoon of cultural normality. A woman carrying highly volcanic energy— an artist, a manic-depressive, a troubled genius—will offer a child greater highs and lows, peaks of creative inspiration and emotional closeness balanced by lows of frightening instability and frosty indifference. A woman offering highly fractured, unstable, low vibrational energy—a drug-addicted teenager with no interest in a child—will offer a childhood of apathy and neglect.

This vibrational energy flows in a constant stream from your bodies, particularly your heads. It can be detected by nonphysical consciousnesses focusing on physical life, searching among the clouds of vibrational energy for sympathetic pattern. Since souls still bound to the human cycle also carry a vibrational pattern carrying the imprint of their prior incarnational experiences, most often a link is made between parent and soul-child carrying sympathetic patterns.

If you think of the families you know, doesn't it seem that the parents and children are on essentially the same wavelength—that creative parents raise creative children; harsh, indifferent parents raise uptight, emotionally repressed children; intellectual parents raise bright, verbal children, and so on. Of course (we anticipate your objection), you conclude that the child turns out this way because of his parents' approach. Certainly a parent acts as a filter—activating some potentials, suppressing others—but a child's innate nature will struggle to manifest no matter how contrary the parental strictures.

For you may also know of "born survivors," children miraculously emerging from appalling childhood experiences with their loving nature, trust, and emotional vitality intact. Here, a deliberately contrarian approach to parental choice has been selected as a means of accelerating growth—for if one can survive such a neglectful childhood and still emerge into an emotionally rich, active, productive adulthood, so much greater is the triumph and growth won by the soul.

Conversely, a loving, emotionally healthy couple may raise a "bad seed," a primitive soul unable to respond to and meet the parents' level of emotional maturity. Here, parents and child make a prebirth pact: defying the common rule of "like attracts like," the parents seek growth through struggling with a child's insolence and indifference to their love, while the primitive soul will be pulled to the upper limit of its emotional potential.

Any system of human psychology which excludes this prebirth selection between parent and child will be incomplete. Parents, trained to believe they receive a tabula rasa at birth, blame themselves when the child fails to live up to expectations, engages in inexplicable behavior, or scorns their love and moral example. Conversely, a mainstream couple may be delighted to raise a genius in the arts, sciences, or human relationships, a sublime ideal of human potential. In both cases, the parents are mystified as to how they begot such a being—where did those qualities come from? As long as the focus remains at the biographical level—from birth onward—the mystery will remain.

Since the purpose of human life is growth through challenge, it stands to reason that the parent-child relationship will be set up to offer challenges that pull both parent and child into new growth. Whether struggling with a rebellious or physically handicapped child, watching in awe as a genius sprouts to full potential, or simply knowing the ineffable tender love a parent feels for a child, the parent-child relationship is often the source of greatest growth in a lifetime.

The parent-child link is made long before birth, when the soul searching earthward for a potential nest evaluates the streams of vibrational energy pouring from the hearts and minds of women. If a karmic relationship is involved the choice will already have been made, and the evaluation will consider only whether the woman's present condition offers potential growth sympathetic with the soul's life purpose. Where no karmic relationship carries over, evaluation is made based on the soul's need—for a contrarian childhood, a close sympathy between parent and child, or as a quiescent launching pad for brilliance.

The Child's Hidden Agenda

The debate over "nature vs. nurture" reveals that, at least to some extent, your culture grants validity to the principle that a child is born with innate personality traits, talents, skills; you edge closer to accepting that sexual orientation is present at birth. While granting that such qualities may be inborn, the cultural dismissal of reincarnation and prelife planning forces this awareness into genetics—that somehow the chromosomes scramble to produce a Mozart, a Picasso, a Schweitzer; that, in fact, such brilliant archetypes of human potential must be genetically abnormal!

Let us move past science's narrow focus to embrace the larger picture. Each of you is the irreducible spark of intent of your higher self, that body of consciousness hovering above the space-time continuum, planting seeds of intent in the fertile soil of human diversity at those times and places most conducive to the higher self's desired experience. At this level of consciousness, linear time does not exist and the sweep of human history pulsates with eternal vitality, offering an infinite range of potential experience.

At this level, the notion of reincarnation as a soul's steady progression over historical time, of a primitive soul gradually attaining enlightenment as the centuries roll by, is incomplete for it presupposes that the soul is locked into the flow of linear time which encases physical experience. Rather, the higher self, hovering outside of time, can scatter seeds of intent attuned to greater or lesser degrees of spiritual wisdom throughout the historical sweep. Whatever your current state of spiritual maturity, there may well be lifetimes planted in your historical future that are pegged to a lower rung on the ladder of enlightenment.

So each of you carries an inborn range of spiritual potential, meaning no matter how severe your childhood there are acts of barbarism to which you will not stoop, and no matter how sublimely nurturing your parents, still there is a ceiling on your potential spiritual growth.

Riding atop this inborn spiritual range, each soul carries a particular "prism" through which it experiences life. You are physical, mental, emotional, and spiritual beings. By prism, we mean that each person focuses his or her life energy through one of these four qualities of human life; one quality will dominate and the others serve as background. Athletes and dancers choose the physical focus. Those happiest amid throngs of friends and family carry the emotional focus. Intellectuals, scholars, writers and incurable readers filter life through their minds. And, rarest of all, those who enjoy deep inner peace, carry no attachments to worldly goods or power, and seek only to live in harmony with the natural and human worlds, focus life through the spiritual prism.

We mention these influences on human personality—karmic bonds, the choice of parents, an inborn range of spiritual potential, and the prism through which life is filtered—only to underscore how rich a tapestry is the soul of the babe fresh from the womb. No tabula rasa here! A child is born with his life purpose, soul agenda, and desired growth experiences fully formed and eager to splash out across the ensuing decades.

So often parents carry a "proper child paradigm" in their heads, a rigid set of ideas as to what constitutes an acceptable child. Most often, such parents seek to vicariously achieve through their children what they failed to achieve in their own youth; or they may be so blinded by economic imperative that only those achievements engraved in the path to economic success—good grades, obedience to authority, suppression of "superfluous" artistic abilities, top of the high school class, top of the college class—meet with parental approval and love.

Every child carries his or her own agenda, life tasks, and desired growth. Left alone, the child will naturally weave a tapestry of private experience from the parental and social web. The young child, still attuned to the pulse of the natural world and immune to economic imperative, is busy every waking moment fashioning physical models of his inner storms and fires, building replicas of his inner life through play, song, and relations to others.

The parent's task is to provide a safe and secure environment for exploration, offer materials for play, be available for support, answer queries, and then *get out of the way*. A parent must respect that the child is a unique soul born with his own purpose and soul potential, pulled effortlessly toward experiences conducive to his growth, and that any attempt to steer the child into socially or parentally approved patterns robs the child of his life purpose.

We do not advocate raising barbarians. We do not mean to suggest that simple manners, common courtesy, and acts of consideration for others not be inculcated by the parents: they must. Rather, we speak of the broader and more damaging crippling of the child's psyche, wrenching a young round soul into a square peg, holding academic or athletic achievement as the sole mark of a child's meaning and value.

Unconditional love—so rarely known—makes no demands, sets no goals, examines no report cards, expects nothing, demands nothing. Unconditional love establishes a secure nest for exploration to which the child can retreat after bruising encounters with the larger world, and in which the child is loved and cherished simply for *being*, not for doing. Unconditional love releases, frees, allows. Unconditional love is the motive force of nature—observe animals with their young—and when flowing from human parent to child, it sparks to life all the child's innate potential and growth without impairment or limitation.

Affection as Vibrational Teaching

When you consider the staggering diversity of the human species—from "primitive" tribes in the equatorial jungles, to western culture's technological sophistication, to peoples eking survival from the harsh permafrost of the north—consider for a moment the extraordinary "winnowing" process any human child must pass through to narrow this tremendous potential into one cultural framework. Every culture has its boundaries and limits of technological, spiritual, and social acceptability, its unique taboos, freedoms, blindness, and so on.

Consider for a moment that your deepest cultural tenets are never directly addressed, never verbalized. When is the last time you heard someone tell a child, "We only think in linear terms" or "Only the physically perceivable has validity" or "Isolation is the basis of our culture"? Yet these are the ideational bricks and mortar of your society. How, then, are they imparted to the young child in his diffuse, unfocused, wide-open adaptability, so that he too narrows his focus to harmonize with his cultural framework?

Through touch, through affection. Each of you emits a steady stream of vibrational information carrying both private material—karmic bleedthrough, biographical memories, future potential—and the cultural framework within which you express your inner life. A given life task will be expressed far differently in a native tribe than in upper class western society, will be reshaped to fit within the parameters of acceptable thought and behavior. So your aura, the energy field swirling about you, blends your private purpose with your cultural framework.

A newborn baby's greatest need is to anchor to his present life. The soul's bond to the body is diffuse and slippery, frequently drifting out during sleep to review prelife planning or a prior lifetime. Upon awaking, a child frequently cries in the hope that he will be held up against someone's (preferably Mom's) chest. Not only does he receive physical nourishment at the breast, but the child drinks in waves of energy swirling about his mother, apprising him of who she is, the flavor of her thoughts, the worldview of her culture, and so on.

The neonate's energy field—a diffuse, amorphous swirl amenable to growth toward Pygmy, Aleut, or Republican— soaks up the maternal vibrations as a means of tethering the child to a specific time and place. Those who handle a small child literally sculpt the child's energy field in harmony with their vibrations, offering the child the security of knowing that he is being welcomed into a given culture, and molding the child's limitless potential into one narrow cultural framework.

You know that infants suffering from lack of affection often evince a "failure to thrive," a failure to grow and mature as they should even if physical nourishment is adequate. The milk alone is only part of an infant's needs—it simply sustains the physical life of the body—while affection and touch stimulate the emotional, mental, and spiritual dimensions of a child's being.

In many cultures, infants are in constant contact with their mothers, carried in slings or other devices as mothers tend to their daily chores. Of all native wisdom, this is the highest: *an infant needs a steady stream of affectional touch, the ideal being 24 hours a day.*

You see now how the theme of separation, the basis of western culture, is inculcated in your children without ever being openly mentioned: most infants are touched and cuddled far less than they need. Rather than learning bonding, communion, connection, and warmth, they learn separation, isolation, distance, and coolness. From the first day of life, as the infant's need to tether himself to his caretakers, and through them their cultural framework, is only partially filled, the child's psyche atrophies in a way, never pulsing into full, rich vitality. An entire life is lived as if under a haze, reducing life's brilliantly hued potentials to muted pastels.

Boys are hit hardest by this process, for it is not "manly" to need others, to share affection, to cry in another's arms. If anything, boys need affection more than girls, for man's focus is on the material world while woman's is on the spiritual aspects of life. In order to balance the risky potentials of an excessively material focus, the spiritual element of a man's psyche—his "feminine" side—must be boosted to the upper reach of its potential. This happens when a boy is touched and held and hugged constantly, never assaulted with strictures like "Boys don't cry" or "Be a man."

Even older children—boys *and* girls—are healthiest wrapped in a warm cocoon of affectional touch. As they grow older and take control of their bodies, they will determine when they need such contact and will naturally seek it out. Perhaps the most effective way of exchanging energy at the auric level is to sleep together—to share a nap or a night in bed with an adult. In sleep, when the sharp physical focus is released and you become your true selves, the exchange of energy between auric fields is accelerated and enriched. The child of whatever age still needs to soak up adult energy—learning what it means to be a man or woman in your culture—and this is achieved effortlessly and most effectively in the sleep state.

So many of your culture's troubles—lonely, isolated adults; youths seeking affection through sex; men's inability to truly bond; your estrangement from nature; brutal sports; private striving at the expense of the larger community—have their genesis in infants not held enough, children told not to cry, children's bodies violated in painful punishment (*any* infliction of pain, however slight, is a violation). When you gaze at the world around you and wonder how it ever came to this—look no further than the sterile and impartial bonding most infants suffer, permanently stunting their ability to connect, bond, nurture, and love.

The bond between parent and child is your most sacred. When cherished and respected as such, the parent weaves a warm, safe space for exploration, showering the child with love and affection, yet respecting the child's private agenda and growth. To heal your lives, to heal your world—begin here, with happy, vibrant children secure in their bond to natural and human worlds, with their ability to love and connect whole and intact. From such young ones will come the new order for which you so yearn.

The Abortion Debate:
Its Deeper Meaning

As the flow of daily events in an individual's life rides atop deeper unseen currents, so can communal events be understood as symbolic expressions of themes and issues emerging from the collective unconscious. On both individual and mass levels, those events carrying great emotional impact derive their energy from the friction sparked as psychic structures are built up and torn down, grating against each other in the private or communal psyche. During times of great upheaval—private or collective—the clash between incompatible psychic structures spills into symbolic expression as highly charged events.

As western culture's traditional mechanistic, soulless worldview collapses into the multifarious global crisis, an ascendent worldview struggles to rise into awareness and right the course. The disparity between the two cosmologies is so great, and the urgency of the crisis so compelling, that the schism between the two worldviews roils with energy, cascading into symbolic expression as communal events of passionate intensity.

Because the battle over abortion resembles just that—a battle, a war—and because it evokes such fervent passions on both sides of the issue, abortion stands as one of the key symbols of the friction between the ascending new worldview and the declining old worldview. With that understanding, we can view abortion as though through a prism, examining each theme or color which blends into the white-heat battle of "pro-life" versus "pro-choice."

The Fetus As Symbol:
The Fear Driving the "Pro-Life" Camp

As mentioned above, social issues of great emotional intensity are often symbolic expressions of eruptions in the collective unconscious. The more hysterical, rigid, and uncompromising a person or group is in advocating a position, the greater the chance that the advocacy is but the surface expression of deeper issues with which the person or group is grappling. In the case of the "pro-life" side of the abortion debate, we find perhaps the shrillest, most uncompromising, most militant advocates of any social issue. More, we find apparent contradictions and hypocrisy; as, for example, in those who claim "sanctity of life" as their motive while bombing abortion clinics.

When surface contradictions appear, fear is at work. Indeed, it is fear, not respect for the sanctity of life, that fuels the "pro-life" camp. Let us look briefly at the nature of fear and its manifestations.

Behind every irrational fear lies an erroneous belief. Erroneous beliefs are those contrary to reality, and irrational fears are the outer coatings on such beliefs. Most often such belief-fear couplings are carried as psychic scars from childhood, where one's innate self-love and trust in the world's safety have been perverted. Obscuring the erroneous belief behind an irrational fear makes difficult an accurate assessment of one's fundamental beliefs; in addition, fears often further mask their true source by latching onto entirely disparate beliefs.

Here is the source of the apparent contradictions and hypocrisy in those motivated by fear. Because fears seek psychic strength by attaching themselves to disparate beliefs, those beliefs may well contradict each other or cancel each other out. The fear masking itself behind the contradictory beliefs is the unifying nexus, binding the contradictory values in an irrational, jumbled stew of hypocrisy.

As another aspect of the nature of fear, it is a psychological maxim that inner conflicts and fears which are too frightening to openly acknowledge and accept may be projected onto others, onto the world at large, as a way of gaining distance from them and therefore dealing with them in a safer, more oblique manner. This defense mechanism of "projection" allows one to deal with inner conflicts at arm's length, avoiding the intensity of probing introspection.

These principles help us to understand the motivations of the "pro-life" camp. For here we find a shrill, impassioned group railing against the slaughter of "preborn children," while engaging in the apparent hypocrisy of ignoring the needs and rights of *already born* women and children, with some even engaging in violence carrying the potential for severe harm.

When surface contradictions appear, fear is at work. What beliefs do the "pro-life" forces hold? First, most base their actions on a traditional, often fundamentalist, Christianity. The Old Testament Jehovah was the world's first dysfunctional parent, alternately blessing and condemning His human creations, drowning the race when it dissatisfied Him, demanding infanticide of Abraham as proof of obeisance.

To believe in the Jehovah model of a creator, then, is to live in perpetual fear of a wrathful, vengeful creator figure who has the power and the will to snuff out the lives of those who displease Him. One feels tiny, frail, and helpless, a mere insect under God's stern and unforgiving gaze—and heel. While Jesus' later teachings were meant to steer the race toward an image of a God of love and forgiveness, conservative

Christians tend to cling to the Old Testament Jehovah as the model of their creator.

Consider the fetus. It is tiny, frail, and helpless. It is utterly dependent on its mother, forever at her mercy, incapable of independent action or freeing itself from her omnipotent control. The mother-fetus relationship thus symbolically represents the relationship between conservative Christian and Jehovah. And because one hesitates to do battle against a wrathful and omnipotent God—a prudent choice!—the inner conflict is projected outward, onto the world at large, onto the fetuses floating in their helpless dependency. Here the fundamentalist can finally do battle against the secretly despised creator figure. Here millennia of chafing under the creator's capricious omnipotence can finally be rectified.

The act of abortion is an exquisitely precise enactment of the fundamentalist's greatest fear, that of being snuffed out by a creator figure. The mother—exercising her life-and-death power—chooses to terminate a pregnancy and the fetus is destroyed during the abortion procedure. It is the fundamentalist's horror: an omnipotent decision to end a life followed by an act of lethal violence against a tiny and helpless being. Abortion thus becomes a gruesome drama scripted by the fundamentalist's darkest nightmares.

As mentioned, fears often latch onto beliefs far removed from their genuine source. In this case, a fear born of a belief in one's impotent helplessness instead trumpets the "sanctity of life" as its basis. But beliefs fueled by fear always reveal themselves in the end by hypocrisies and contradictions.

Where is the respect for the "sanctity of life" in forcing women to bring unwanted babies to term? Where is the respect for the "sanctity of life" in further crowding a grossly overpopulated planet? Where is the respect for the "sanctity of life" in attacking, berating, threatening, even assaulting those involved in the abortion procedure? The apparent hypocrisy reveals that the "pro-life" camp is motivated not by respect for life but by fear, fear projected outward and symbolically enacted by a mother choosing to end a pregnancy.

This explains the hysteria, the fury, the rigid, uncompromising stance, the willingness to suffer arrest and prison, to defy the authorities, to commit verbal and physical violence: The "pro-life" forces are not battling for the lives of the unborn. They are battling for their own lives.

The Pro-Choice Camp:
The Goddess Emerges

Although the pro-choice side of the abortion debate is not fueled by sublimated fear as is the "pro-life" camp, still the pro-choice advocacy of a "woman's right to control her body" is but the surface expression of a deeper undercurrent flowing beneath society. We may refer to this ascendent system of values as the emerging "Goddess principle."

Most readers will already be familiar with the Goddess concept, a growing body of thought digging deep into humanity's roots for evidence of a time when the feminine principles of inclusion, compassion, and harmony between the sexes governed human affairs. Yet this anthropological probing is itself another expression of a still deeper shift occurring in the species' collective unconscious.

Western culture has for millennia been dominated by the patriarchy principle, a system ruled by predominantly masculine values of competition, violence, and dominance. As this system plays itself out, manifesting as a world torn by war, poverty, and impending ecological catastrophe, the system's spiritual barrenness becomes apparent. As humanity casts about for a fresh philosophical framework to right its course, long-suppressed bodies of thought percolate into awareness.

The emerging interest in Goddess religions and cultures reflects the deeper understanding that western culture's core malaise results from its disregard for feminine spiritual principles. At base, the difference between the sexes is this: man is the material keeper of the world; woman is the spiritual keeper of the world. Only a harmonious, respectful blend of these energies and perspectives results in a healthy, just, sane world.

So the pro-choice rallying cry of a woman's right to control her own body is, in fact, one narrow slice of the deeper emergence of the Goddess principle, a worldview which cherishes and upholds *everyone's* freedom and dignity, not just those of the pregnant woman. The pro-choice forces are the front-line soldiers in the larger struggle to restore western culture to its neglected spiritual roots.

The Morality of Abortion: When Does "Human Life" Begin?

If all life is sacred, is abortion murder? Are embryos to be considered "preborn children," as the "pro-life" forces claim? At what point does a fetus become "human"? When does a soul attach itself to the growing fetus?

Such questions can never be resolved among the various political, scientific, and religious camps debating the abortion issue, as there is no agreement on fundamental beliefs and values. We offer our perspective from the spiritual dimension, where the process of a soul linking with a human body is perhaps more clearly understood.

No life exists without consciousness; indeed, consciousness precedes corporal form. Without consciousness infusing a living being, it soon decays into a heap of inorganic elements. A growing fetus can be sufficiently infused with consciousness by its mother that there is no necessity for a "soul," a distinct sprout of consciousness, to link with the child in utero. In fact, in some cases a soul does not link with a child until after birth. "Crib death syndrome" is frequently a result of a child born without a soul having "claimed" it as the vehicle for earthly exploration.

Given this understanding, as a general rule a soul "links" with a fetus between the third and ninth months of pregnancy. As the fetus grows and the pregnancy takes on increasing importance to the mother, her thoughts increasingly fill with plans and expectations for the new life she carries. As a woman's thoughts focus more intently on her growing child, her thought process ripples to the level of consciousness where those souls eager for earthly life can perceive and evaluate it. Based on the degree of congruence between a soul's life purpose and the expected childhood experiences to be offered by a particular mother, the match is made.

For this reason, a woman who becomes pregnant through accident or assault, who has no desire or means to raise a child, and who therefore contemplates abortion, will radiate a starkly different thought process regarding the fetus she carries. No soul seeking a lifetime commitment to earth would link with the fetus growing inside such a woman. The process is self-selecting and occurs on a level of consciousness beyond the normal waking focus.

The question of when a fetus becomes "human," and whether abortion is therefore murder, simply reflects ignorance of the process through which souls link with their earthly bodies. From the perspective of the soul level of consciousness, one can no more "murder" an unselected fetus than one can "murder" an inanimate object. Murder is the deliberate destruction of life; and where no life infuses a tiny fetus, abortion entails no violation.

The Old Order's Last Gasp

Abortion has been legal in America since 1973. Why, then, have the anti-abortion forces risen to prominence in the Eighties and Nineties? Why have the protests, blockades, and harassment reached a fever pitch in the last few years, with the descent into "justifiable homicide" cutting down abortion providers?

As mentioned earlier, social issues fraught with passion and polemic are fueled by the friction between conflicting worldviews, one decaying, the other ascending. Each of the last three decades has served as a phase in the four-step process of cultural revolution. The Sixties saw the initial burst of energy infusing society with a fresh vision and vitality, chipping away at the edifice of white male patriarchy. The Seventies was the decade of rest and reflection, when the legacy of the Sixties was sifted through and evaluated, to retain what was truly of value and permanence while discarding the excess and harm of the Sixties' rougher edges. In the Eighties, society was once again infused with a fresh burst of energy, this time to set the stage, in clear and unmistakable terms, for the "time of trial," the struggle between the declining old order and the ascending new order now unfolding in the Nineties.

Like a fire throwing off a few final sparks before decaying to cold ash, a philosophy or worldview whose time has passed will be infused with a final burst of energy as it grinds against its successor worldview. This process became apparent in the Eighties with the rise of the right wing in politics and religion, and accelerates in the Nineties with political power shifting toward the conservative side. For all its apparent strength, the right wing's growth is best understood as the rise before the fall, a final hoisting of the flag and beating of the drums before surrendering to the inevitable ascendence of a new worldview and way of life.

This process takes place on levels beyond human affairs as well, as the Eighties witnessed evidence of appalling ecological developments, including holes in the ozone layer, unabated rain forest destruction, the unprecedented droughts, temperature extremes, and storms of uncommon frequency and severity. The earth itself plays a part in the schism between old and new orders as it presents in starkest terms the choice between perpetuating the old-order approach to nature—inevitably leading to complete ecological collapse—or embracing a new approach based on respect for nature's wisdom and sanctity.

Thus the anti-abortion forces have risen to prominence in the Eighties and Nineties as an expression of the growing showdown between old and new orders. By synthesizing old-order religion—a Bible-based belief in an omniscient, capricious creator figure—and old-order conservative politics, the anti-abortion forces serve as mouthpieces for the decaying worldview as it grinds against the ascending new order.

The Nineties witness the opening salvos of the "time of trial," when the trends of the prior three decades erupt into fierce social conflict. Either the new worldview is embraced, leading to ecological and social restoration, or the old order triumphs at the expense of a habitable planet and social cohesion. The abortion debate plays an invaluable role in the process, standing as it does as a symbol for the deeper upheavals occurring in the collective unconscious.

Abortion as a Social Crucible

We have examined abortion from several perspectives, all with an eye toward unearthing the deeper societal currents flowing beneath the protest marches and stinging rhetoric. As mentioned before, any social issue engendering passionate emotion and fervent debate derives its energy from the grinding schism between two opposing worldviews, one ascending and one decaying. Abortion is a rich metaphor for the emergence of the new order, for it weaves together questions of the meaning and sanctity of life; social control versus individual freedom; the Judeo-Christian legacy of an omnipotent, wrathful God, hidden beneath the "pro-life" camp's hysteria; the emergence of the "Goddess," a life-affirming, inclusive, compassionate spirituality; and it illumines the fractured philosophical underpinning of western culture, as scientific, religious, and political worldviews clash in antagonistic conflict over these vital issues.

As mountains rise inexorably from the sea, so is humanity carried to ever greater heights of spiritual understanding. The clash between the old order and the new order is best viewed not as a struggle between worldviews of equal strength and validity, but as the furious dying assault of the decaying old order railing against the emerging new order. The rise of the right wing in general can best be understood as the deathbed shudders of the dying old order, struggling to its elbows for a few final blasts of reactionary protest before succumbing to the ineluctable emergence of the new order.

Abortion is a crucible in which this struggle takes place; it reduces the deeper process to a manageable, symbolic expression. The battle over abortion is thus best viewed as one strand of the greater social tapestry being woven as the old order's decaying thread is replaced with the vibrant fiber of a culture living in harmony with nature's principles.

Questions and Answers

We receive many letters seeking Alexander's perspective or advice on a wide variety of issues. As space allows, he replies to these inquiries in *The Alexander Journal*.

❖   ❖   ❖

"What is the process through which a discarnate entity such as Alexander communicates his thoughts to us?"

To understand how a nonphysical consciousness expresses itself in human language, first consider that the process is identical for all beings, whether in human form or not. That is, a thought exists first as a preverbal unit of consciousness, an amorphous swirl of information. Human infants and animals have thoughts and emotions, for example, but lacking the ability to squeeze thought into symbolic language, they express their thoughts through direct action. If you consider the times when words failed to adequately express an emotion or experience, you realize that words are but the symbolic coating on an experience which exists in full vibrancy only on the preverbal level of consciousness.

Given this understanding, it is no great leap to understand the process through which nonphysical entities "speak" through their human hosts. Behind every word of every human language lies a preverbal thought-form of which the word is the symbolic expression. "Cat" in English and "gato" in Spanish differ in their symbolic expression, but the preverbal thought-form they represent remains identical. So an entity feeding a stream of thought through a human host need only link with the host's consciousness in a trance state; as the host's consciousness accelerates and the entity's thought-forms decelerate, a link is made through which thought-form assumes the symbolic expression of the host's native language.

No entity "speaks" in any human language. We offer our material in nonverbal form, which is then translated by the host's consciousness. As a result, the precision and eloquence of a given entity is controlled by the linguistic fluency of the host. Writers frequently make excellent channels, for their love of language ensures a smooth, accurate translation of the material. By the same token, channels whose command of language is not as strong may appear to give voice to entities needing a course in remedial grammar. Again, it is the host's facility with language that determines the verbal expression of the entity's material.

In a sense, entities may "study" English or other host languages, for as there are great differences among human cultures, so are those differences reflected in their languages. Each culture carries its fundamental worldview as the foundation of its verbal and written expression. Some cultures offer deep, rich, varied expressions for emotional content, while others excel in highly technical jargon. So an entity choosing to speak through a particular host may study the basics of the host's language for an understanding of the parameters through which material will be delivered. But, again, the specific words and phrases produced will be determined solely on the host's side of the exchange.

❖   ❖   ❖

(Submitted by a *Journal* reader at the height of California's recent drought):

"Do you care to comment on the drought?"

Any discussion of weather and natural events must be based on two principles of human influence in its creation. First, the mass human consciousness can be thought of as a "cloud" or blanket of consciousness covering the globe and contributing either stability or instability to the extant energy patterns. While the human species does not alone control the weather, you can influence it. It is interesting to note that areas of great political and social turmoil seem to suffer an unusually high proportion of natural disasters. Such are not directly caused by human consciousness—the larger earth features have been in place far longer than human society—but the timing of great movements of earth can be influenced by an unstable human society.

The second human contribution to weather and natural events is the electrification of the globe and its concomitant disturbance of the global "immune system," the checks and balances holding weather patterns in steady consistency. Because natural forces like sun, wind, and rain formation are largely electromagnetic events, the electrification of the globe poses great danger to the earth's capacity to regulate itself.

It is not that the West is doomed to permanent drought. The point is that the normal pattern has been disrupted by human activity, so the earth cannot follow its historical pattern. Everything is thrown off balance, so alternating years of drought and monsoon may replace the tradition of regular winter storms of consistent, predictable magnitude.

Drought, then, is one extreme on the weather continuum, finding expression because the earth's immune system is crippled by human interference. Looking beyond the West, other areas may find winters growing colder and summers hotter, rains heavier or lighter, and "freak" natural events occurring with greater frequency.

❖   ❖   ❖

"I'd like it if Alexander would tell us how we, in our individual selves, can fundamentally change our culture. I got the feeling from Journal *#7 that there wasn't a thing that I could do myself to help. That composting, etc. was a joke."*

The question contains its own answer—since society is made up of individuals, it will change as individuals change. Our *Journal* article referred to the strength and tenacity of "old order" thinking at this time and its potential for increasing danger and repression as the foundations of the old order crumble. Against the seemingly immense power of government and business, the individual may indeed feel powerless and believe that individual action is of no consequence.

Since mass events are reflections of mass consciousness, it follows that the most powerful influence one can have on the world's events is to change one's consciousness—or, if one is already centered and acting from a pure heart, to become a visible example to others. This can appear so impotent—like those who simply held candles in silence to protest the Gulf War—and yet this apparent weakness simply underscores that your society considers power only in physical terms: numbers of tanks, warplanes, machine guns, bombs. Is this where true power lies? Is this how Gandhi ended British rule, or Martin Luther King the grip of institutionalized racism?

Only a soulless culture, bereft of a genuine spiritual life, would consider power solely in physical terms. For the material world is simply the medium, the tools, through which you express your consciousness. True power, genuine power, therefore lies in consciousness, in the heart and mind. Ideas are the true building blocks of your culture, as every weapon first existed in someone's mind, as did every nonviolent protest or boycott. Consciousness is primary, its physical expression only a reflection.

So to change your world, you start with yourself. Against the power and influence of huge chemical companies and agribusiness, carrying your coffee grounds to the compost pile may indeed appear impotent. Growing your own food without chemicals, working in partnership with nature, may seem of little consequence. Yet this is where you must start, and from your acts will slowly radiate a new way of thinking and living that those edging toward growth will notice. Some will ask you how to compost, or why you do it. Some will inquire about organic gardening. When you offer your knowledge and enthusiasm, you light a spark in another's heart. From such sparks grow revolutions.

So composting is no joke, no well-meaning exercise in futility. It is an acknowledgement of your devotion to maintaining the cycle of life, returning your food waste to the earth whence it came, there to nourish next year's crop. And as you influence those around you, you send out ripples of higher consciousness, overlapping with other ripples, creating a lattice of consciousness which grows in power as more are awakened. From such small, private acts will be woven the fabric of a new society.

❖   ❖   ❖

"Alexander emphasizes the west's harmful exaggeration of separations. I wonder if the Chinese-like civilizations of East Asia may not suffer from exaggerations of group (families, etc.) controls which smother the individual excessively and, hence, a mixture of the two might not produce a better, healthier balance than either one separately—which may be happening now. Or should I conclude Alexander thinks such Asian civilizations are much superior?"

We consider no culture superior to any other; we only point out that some live in relative harmony with natural law while others violate it almost as a matter of principle. Western culture, of course, falls into the latter category.

The world is moving in two seemingly disparate directions: one toward narrowing tribal identity, particularly evident in the former Eastern Bloc countries whose previous unity, enforced by gun and tank, now crumbles to reveal millennia-old ethnic animosities: this is a narrowing of tribal affiliation from the national political level to circles based on common blood or religious heritage.

At the same time, another trend emerges: a growing global consciousness, a loosening of narrow tribal affiliations to embrace the global community. Like all social evolution, this can be achieved through clear-sighted progressive thought or be forced by disaster. Having chosen the latter course, you face the ecological crisis forcing a growing awareness of the interdependence of all life and the urgent need for cooperation beyond national borders. Acid rain respects no borders; neither does radiation or global warming. Only a cooperative effort by all nations will prevent the more traumatic results of these ominous trends.

Another element of growing global consciousness is the mass media, allowing instantaneous transmission of art and information. This enhances the progress toward a world of shared understanding and mutual respect.

Each of the great races has taken a particular focus on human life. You move now toward an integrative era, blending these long-disparate strands into a new humanity built upon the strengths of each racial heritage. Asian cultures have emphasized group, tribe, family, at the expense of individual identity, while western culture has enshrined the rugged individual as its archetype. Both cultural frameworks, running to excess, cripple the hope of reaching life's highest potential.

It is no accident that the western world now hears much of "community" from political and spiritual leaders; the intentional communities movement deliberately abandons the rugged individual archetype in favor of group living. At the same time, Asian cultures, particularly young people, slough off the rigid patterns and expectations of the group imperative in favor of greater personal freedom and expression.

Over time, of course, these two great strands will blend into a global culture upholding the supremacy of the individual but embedding the individual within a familial or tribal context, a communal stability and warmth. The ultimate goal, of course, is a global humanity valuing "diversity within unity," cherishing the unique attributes of diverse cultures while identifying most strongly with the common blood flowing in every human vein.

❖   ❖   ❖

Two related questions:

"I would like to learn more about the relationship of humans and animals—what do our companion animals think and feel about the world and us? What is their link to All That Is? What do animals who are raised to be eaten think of the whole matter? What happens to them when they die?"

"Given the sacrament which exists between man and animals, why is vegetarianism not embraced in response to the horrible conditions of factory farming—given that life flows with you, not against you in pursuit of positive goals, why is it so difficult to make animal rights a fact in this society?"

As mammalian consciousness divides into the multitude of fleshbound forms, each strand takes a particular focus and limitations, choosing to concentrate in a certain geographical range, to live as groups or in solitude, to eat vegetation or other animals, and so on. As each strand increasingly specializes, making it more distinct, the natural tendency is to narrow affiliation to one's own tribe, to live in the distilled essence of that unique focus. Animals rarely interact across species lines beyond the predator-prey relationship.

So companion animals are an aberration in the natural world, an intertwining of consciousness and common welfare between man and those species amenable to pethood. Over time, the mutual dependency increases and such animals lose their wild edge, their aptitude for living in the wild. In a sense, both animal and human consciousness are altered, creating a "bridge" consciousness across which interspecies exchange takes place.

What animals lose by becoming companions is their wildness, their instinctual ease in the natural world. What they gain is relationship—bonds of love and affection of a different flavor than that shared within a species. They gain entrance into human community, becoming part of a family and its vicissitudes.

So the consciousness behind companion animals is twofold: first, to stretch beyond instinct into affiliations of love and loyalty with another species; second, to "study" the human species from the perspective of a wet nose and wagging tail. Just as you find exotic human tribes of great interest, and may enjoy visiting them in their native habitat, so does "companion animal consciousness" offer insight into human nature from a radically different slant than is available from human consciousness. In fact, an oversoul focusing on human experience may project an offshoot or two into life as companion animals, thus enriching and rounding out the total human experience. (This does not mean that human souls reincarnate as animals, but that's another volume!)

Now, regarding animals raised to be eaten. As implausible as it may seem, there is little weight given at the level of consciousness to death at the hands of man versus natural death—the end result is the same, the release of earthly form.

So while those bodies of consciousness animating food animals are aware that their lives will be shorter than is natural, this is of tertiary importance in choosing corporal form. Of greatest importance is the expected experience while in flesh, not the likely nature of death. So the choice between "food animal" and "wild animal" is, in itself, of little weight.

At the level of consciousness, it is understood that consciousness is eternal and immutable while earthly forms flow in and out of existence through the cycle of birth and death. At the level of consciousness, little distinction is drawn between eating plants and eating animals—in both cases, the essential energy and consciousness are released from their earthly form and that form is then consumed. It is natural law that you must consume other life to sustain your own. This is not a cause for sadness, but simply a recognition of nature's grand cycle, whereby discarded bodies sustain bodies still vital.

This is not to say there aren't wise reasons for avoiding meat in your particular time and place, given the brutal treatment of factory farm animals, the concentration of pesticide residues in flesh, and so on. But from the level of consciousness, scant distinction is drawn between consuming plant or animal food; both are elements of the natural cycle.

The struggle for animal rights is one facet of the larger dynamic between old and new orders now playing out across the whole of your culture. At base, the struggle is between the Judeo-Christian heritage with its alleged dominion of man over animal (in which animals are conveniently devoid of souls) versus a recognition of the divinity immanent in all living beings. As this new awareness struggles toward acceptance, it faces roadblocks placed by those who profit from sustaining the old order. Ultimately, as in all things, the moral cause will prevail; the question is how difficult you will make the transition, how many animals must needlessly suffer and die at your hands, thereby brutalizing your own humanity as well.

❖　　　❖　　　❖

"What of the possibility of a polar (planetary) shift in this probability before the beginning of the next century?"

You will recall that in our response to the previous question about human influence on weather patterns, we discussed how the global human consciousness creates a blanket of energy about the earth, influencing natural events. The notion of "pole shift" is commonly misunderstood to mean that the north and south poles physically trade places, flipping the earth upside down on its axis and raining obvious calamity down on those riding along.

Pole shift can be more accurately understood as a shift in *polarity* of the poles, an electromagnetic event of great power, but not a physical wrenching of the earth on its axis. This shifting has happened before in your earth's history and is part of a larger cycle in which the earth is embedded, a cosmic process whose "waves" take thousands of years to crest. Rather than the picture of a dark void painted by your scientific schooling, the cosmos vibrates at every point with energy and vitality. The whole of the cosmos is bathed by massive electromagnetic fields which, in their natural course, will influence the electromagnetic activity of smaller bodies like the earth.

The anticipation of a pole shift occurring within a decade reflects an attempt to stitch together two vaguely understood but deeply felt processes: this larger cosmic electromagnetic ocean in which you float, and that human society is poised for radical change in the years ahead. Understanding, however unconsciously, that human consciousness influences natural events, you express your anticipation of a major shift in consciousness in physical terms, as a radical uprooting and shifting of the earth's course. Pole shift is a metaphor, then, a way of expressing in concrete terms the dimly sensed revolution in human consciousness which lies ahead.

The human-weather interaction is a two-way street, and cosmic events certainly influence human behavior in ways barely understood. When the massive undulating electromagnetic waves flow through your solar system, the influence on human behavior and culture is profound. So, again, when such a wave approaches, you express your unconscious knowledge with the metaphor of pole shift, an event of great electromagnetic power.

Our sense is that your planet is not due for such an event for at least a century. For all the upheaval of your time, such represents the first sprinkles of an approaching tidal wave which requires many decades to fully play itself out. There may well be a linking of a newly evolved human consciousness with a cosmic wave, each reinforcing and enhancing the other, but you are still in the very early preparatory stages of such a consciousness shift.

So sleep easy—your bedroom is not likely to end up in the South Pacific any time soon!

❖   ❖   ❖

"Why has mankind consistently chosen to allow those in power to distort and misrepresent the teachings given in regard to the primacy of the individual —Christianity in particular, with its lies and half-truths, has resulted in a worldview incapable of enhancing value fulfillment."

Imagine that a renowned physicist visited a third grade classroom and delivered a lecture on quantum physics. After one such lecture, he never returned to follow up or correct the students' misinterpretations of the lesson. As time went on, the students struggled to build a cohesive system of physics based on their incomplete, misunderstood knowledge. Over time, a system of physics would emerge, logically consistent but based on faulty premises, which would be disseminated to younger students as fact, written in stone, not to be questioned: after all, this is based on the teachings of a renowned physicist!

So it is with human spiritual progress. Every culture hosts an avatar from time to time, shining a piercing light through the follies and darkness of his time and place, offering pure wisdom to light the way toward a higher understanding, a right living. After the avatar dies, his followers seek to preserve and disseminate the teachings. To do so requires an organization of like-minded followers.

Playing out over centuries, this original ragtag band of persecuted followers can become a major cultural power. It is ironic, then, that every great spiritual teacher encourages individual spiritual exploration and growth, but to preserve and spread such teachings, organizations must be built, leading inevitably to bureaucracy and stifling of individual spiritual search. The greatest damage occurs when the bureaucracy holds *itself* as the conduit through which mortals must pass to reach reunion with the ultimate—as with the Christian church requiring baptism and last rites to ensure a soul's passage to Heaven.

Religions fail to live up to the teachings of the master because avatars bring pure spiritual truth to a world still populated with souls struggling through darkness. They serve as beacons, guiding lights of truth toward which most can only imperfectly stretch. A bureaucratic religion is like any other bureaucracy: rigid, unyielding, dogmatic, slow to change. As with any human institution, personal aggrandizement and political infighting absorb most of the energy and time of those involved.

One key quality of the New Age now dawning is to restore power where it belongs, with the individual, and to drain it from institutions. How do you accomplish this? Again, you start with yourself: you do not give power away to others. You may read and appreciate the teachings of the great spiritual masters—Jesus, Krishna, Mohammed, Buddha—but you do not then pledge undying allegiance to the institutions which have sprouted in their wake. You seek to fashion your own truth, your own personal spiritual system, one which feels right to you.

Today you witness a great interest in spiritual systems outside the Judeo-Christian heritage: Native American spirituality, eastern religions, wicca, the Goddess, and so forth. These all underscore how inadequate your traditional religious institutions have become, and yet they also demonstrate that the lesson has not yet been fully learned: you still look to other sacred systems in hopes of finding spiritual nourishment for the aching hunger within. Ultimately, such eclectic borrowing from other cultures will leave you unfulfilled, for such systems arose organically in their time and place and cannot be transplanted to 20th-century western culture without distortion.

Since human consciousness can never fully comprehend Absolute Truth, each must fashion his or her personal truth as a blend of great teachings and private experience. We encourage using "inner resonance" as a guide— when a teacher or teaching resonates strongly with you, when it feels true and pure, most likely you can absorb the teaching as the foundation on which to build your private spiritual truth. Joining with others of like mind—who make no claims to omniscience or hidden truth—can enhance the process. We also encourage meditation as a means of accessing the inner self, using its wisdom as a filter through which outside teaching can blend with inner truth.

To conclude, religious bureaucracies inevitably stifle the very individuality their founders championed. The strongest protest you can make is to refuse to surrender your power to any such institution, instead navigating the corridors of spiritual growth with inner resonance as your guide.

❖   ❖   ❖

*"It is not satisfying to only take note of all the develop-
ments of humanity's history (and misery) unless there is a purpose, a plan, conceived in love. There are the Teachings by the
great religious leaders through ages past, who profess love for
mankind, helping, steering from 'above' and from 'within'—
why do you never mention love?"*

For two reasons. One, your culture's definition of love
differs so radically from what we would term genuine love
that we do not care to confuse the two. Our definition of love
is a respect for, and cherishing of, the divine spark in another.
Such respect entails recognition of the uniqueness of each person, the supreme importance of allowing each to tread his
private path, and a refusal to entangle others in webs of possessiveness, jealousy, or personal need.

By this standard, few relationships—parent-child, romantic, friendship—pass the test. Almost always, personal needs
and insecurities infect the relationship with the urge to mold
the other to one's liking, to own the other's time and attention, to exclude outside relationships. Genuine love allows,
sets free, releases, encourages the other to his or her highest
potential. We would therefore rather use the term "respect"
to describe the ideal basis of a relationship, rather than use
"love" with its unhappy connotations.

Second, we do not scatter messages of love throughout
our work because that is not our place or purpose. Whether
addressing you en masse through written material or individually in private session, we offer respect—respect for the
hard work of being human, for your unique and irreplaceable
role in the drama of creation, for your struggle to live up to
your divine potential. It is not our place to offer love in human terms; that is meant to come from others in flesh. We
come as a guide or teacher, filtering our awareness through
our human host, but not as a companion. By any definition, a
loving relationship rides on a foundation of physical affection

and such we cannot offer. For this, you must turn to your comrades-with-arms.

❖   ❖   ❖

"Is there a continuous creation of new souls somewhere in the spirit world, and why would so many souls be created that this planet is driven into overpopulation destruction? This indicates a very unintelligent universe."

First let us address the question of "soul creation," for an understanding of the process through which consciousness attaches itself to human form will illuminate other aspects of the overpopulation question.

Because all time is simultaneous, in deepest terms there is no point of creation for a soul; souls, projections of consciousness, exist in eternal viability within the womb of All That Is. Within your space-time framework, however, All That Is splinters Its consciousness into families of consciousness, oversouls, individual souls, and so on, in Its thirst for an infinite variety of experience. As consciousness splinters in the progression from its ultimate source to that animating one human form, it increasingly specializes, narrowing its focus and range of awareness. While many believe they have souls, or understand the concept of reincarnation and oversouls, such remain cognitive abstractions, thoughts and ideas, rather than experienced realities. The consciousness vitalizing human form turns outward, toward the physical world, for experience and "forgets" its ultimate source.

Each person, each nation, each world, is but one version of an infinite sea of probabilities. The life you recount as your own is simply a fragment of all probable yous swarming in equal validity within their realities. Through your thoughts and beliefs you pull into experience the events of your life, but those events not chosen are played out in other realities by other probable yous. Your life story, your biography, is one small sliver of your greater multidimensional reality.

The same holds true of the earth as well; all possible versions of its history exist in equal validity. The flow of historical events, as you recount them, is one slice of the infinite sea of probable earths existing in eternal validity beyond the space-time framework.

Thus there are probable earths on which the human population never exceeded sustainable limits, and probable earths where human overpopulation has so burdened the ecological balance that rampant starvation and disease force a reduction in population. This latter probability looms ever closer to your experienced reality, a shadow in the recesses of consciousness urging you to avert its horrific suffering through immediate constructive action.

The question of "where all the souls are coming from" as your population mounts thus misses the point. Since all probable earths exist simultaneously, with their varying levels of human population, souls are not "coming from" anywhere, but are merely being drawn into expression within your experienced reality. There is no set number of souls manufactured at some distant dawn of time, nor is there a surplus anxiously awaiting birth. Those projections of consciousness seeking learning and growth through human experience have a literally infinite variety of probable earths and historical time periods from which to choose. To complicate matters, an oversoul can create parallel selves, multiple human forms existing within the same time period, as a means of experiencing a given stretch of history from a variety of standpoints. The maxim "love your neighbor as yourself" takes on new meaning with this understanding!

Our reader remarked on the apparent "unintelligence" of a system which would create so many souls and not enough earthlike planets to put them on, forcing a buildup and resulting in massive starvation. We hope that the above material will offer a new perspective, of the brilliance of the physical system in its infinite probabilities, granting absolute freedom to each person and world to create private and collective realities. The current overpopulation problem and resultant starvation are not due to faulty wisdom on the universe's part, but to western culture's divorce from the natural order.

In nature, each individual and species employs the natural resources immediately at hand. Western culture's technology allows it far greater freedom in its use of natural resources: you can irrigate the desert, extract fossil fuels, use chemicals to increase food production, and transport resources around the globe, allowing you to temporarily step outside of nature's checks and balances. Ultimately, violations of nature will be redressed, either through recognition of the deleterious effects and commitment to change, or through catastrophe.

In the deepest terms, each probable earth is an experiment. The experimental design in your case is to inject a particular slant of human consciousness, the excessive use of reason at the expense of emotion and harmony with nature, and note the results. Will such a system lead to growth and fulfillment for all its creatures? As the experiment has played out, it is apparent that this slant of consciousness, the western worldview, is incompatible with the planet's long-term health. The challenge now, to which you and all others now alive have committed to tackle, is to employ your reason to restore yourselves to living in harmony with nature's principles, to mend your sundered psyches by granting equal validity to their emotional and spiritual components.

Given the extraordinary challenges facing you in the years ahead, and given that the very purpose of human life is to learn and grow through challenge, how could there be a shortage of souls eager to participate? Souls swarm toward historical periods of great upheaval like white blood cells to a wound: for there lies the greatest opportunity for growth, healing, and spiritual progress.

❖　　　❖　　　❖

"Many 'conscious' people face the dilemma of whether to bring children into a world smother under humanity's exploding population. Is it not always a violation to add one more hungry mouth, another future 'consumer,' to the billions already here?"

To some extent it is a violation to bring a child into a world as overpopulated as yours. At the same time, to some extent it is a violation to take a shower when your water supply has been diverted from its proper course. Do you stop taking showers? Is filthiness a badge of holiness?

You must realize that there are certain problems extant in every culture which precede your birth into that culture. While your choice of birth into that culture necessarily entails an agreement to participate in those problem areas, it does not make you personally responsible for solving them to the extent that you suffer or deprive yourself. You make yourself aware of the problems of your community; you do what you can to ameliorate them; you support the efforts of others to combat them; you actively join them if you wish; but you do not engage in self-sacrifice in order to solve problems that others created.

Like attracts like. This fundamental law carries over into the choice of parents. Souls searching about for earth parents will choose those of a similar spiritual development. In other words, a soul which has known only violent and exploitative lifetimes cannot and will not seek out loving and spiritually elevated parents—for there are too many intermediate steps, too many lessons in between, which must be confronted and successfully mastered. Similarly, a spiritually developed spirit would not seek to be born into a violent and chaotic home—for those lessons have already been learned.

For this reason, it is most important that the spiritually aware not cease having children out of concern for the planet's overpopulation. Do you see what would happen as a result? A rise in the ranks of the spiritually inchoate—who never give a moment's thought to the effects of anything they do!—and a decrease in the body of spiritually aware individuals who can lead you out of the morass. If anything, we would encourage those in the New Age community to be fruitful and multiply!

It is true that the world population cannot be sustained at present levels and allow your restoration to the natural order. Things will take care of themselves, and if this involves mass starvation or plagues, so it shall be—not as punishment, but as consequence. Those dying will choose to make a statement with their deaths as a means of alerting you to the larger spiritual issues underlying such plagues and starvation. And you will find, once the human species is restored to the natural order, that such overpopulation will not recur for, like the animals, you will assume your proper place in the overall scheme of things, not allowing your numbers to exceed what can reasonably exist in harmony with the planet.

Beyond Death's Door:
Reunion and Integration

Of all the puzzles and mysteries confounding the human species through the millennia, few remain as vexing, as immune to scientific exploration, and as fear provoking as what lies beyond death of the physical body. Needless to say, reports of those who have made the journey are rare and sketchy! Yet each of you has made the transition many times, and will do so again before the cycle of earthly existence has run its course.

Because we *are* on the other side of the veil, perhaps we can offer material leading to a greater understanding of the soul's progress upon release of physical form, particularly focusing on the complex interwoven relationships between each individual soul and the larger bodies of consciousness of which it is a part.

The Transition

Physical death occurs when the streams of energy binding consciousness, or the soul, to a physical organism are redirected away from the physical medium, back into the nonphysical dimension. This can happen abruptly, as in sudden death, or over a period of days and weeks if a gradual release of earthly form is chosen.

Imagine that each molecule of your body is sustained by a beam of intent from your higher self, that beam of intent being a slender stream of consciousness decelerating in intensity as it approaches the physical plane, slowing to frequencies compatible with earthly life. As you grow from infancy through childhood and youth into old age, certain strands will turn on while others are turning off, literally weaving your body's growth and change by the subtle but incredibly complex interweaving of these strands of intent.

At death, these strands of intent gradually cease blinking into the physical medium. The body's cells and molecules, freed from subjugation to the larger body consciousness, begin to assert their individual natures, leading to decay of the larger organism. This you understand, and is meant only as prologue. The far more fascinating process is what occurs to those strands of intent, for so long bound to your physical form, once their energy is redirected to the nonphysical realm.

What is the Soul?

You recognize that each of you, every living being, has a soul, an eternal and inviolate field of consciousness which animates your being, preceded your birth and will survive physical release. It has been common among many religious traditions to consider the soul as a duplicate of the physical body, and that based upon the moral flavor of your life, this duplicate body will find just reward in the spiritual realm, always retaining its sense of itself as the earthly form to which it was attached for however many years.

A more sophisticated understanding recognizes that growth, change, and evolution are immutable processes played out in all realms of existence, physical and nonphysical, and the notion of a soul either condemned or rewarded for all eternity based on the actions of a few earthly decades would be monstrously unfair as well as numbingly static and sterile. Yet the more sophisticated understanding that the soul is ultimately reabsorbed into greater bodies of consciousness carries with it an uneasiness, that the self you know as you might ultimately be extinguished, lost in the cosmic shuffle. To understand how we can have it both ways—an inviolate, eternal soul and reabsorption into higher entities—let us first look at what constitutes a single human soul.

Each soul is an amalgam of several components or influences, one of them primary and the others secondary. The primary element of each soul is the desire to experience a chosen theme through human form. The human drama offers many such primary themes—isolation vs. intimacy, principle vs. expedience, poverty vs. wealth, love vs. hate, body vs. spirit, and so on. The higher self—that higher body of consciousness riding above the earthly plane and holding all incarnational experiences in simultaneous awareness—generally makes a thematic choice and creates a series of incarnations through which to experience that theme in its every aspect.

It is the *intent* of the higher self to experience the primary theme in your time and place, through your person, that provides the bedrock foundation of the soul. No soul is a blank slate, disinterestedly browsing among the rich potentials of human life; underlying each lifetime is a focused arena of growth, the basic thematic motif through which experience will be filtered.

The next greatest influence on the soul is the life experiences gained from birth onward. Most life themes are enormous canvases upon which can be painted innumerable lifetimes of striking diversity, yet bound together in the common theme. Choosing the time, place, and parents of earth birth narrows this grand potential down to one small corner of the canvas. Consider the vast diversity of the human race in its racial, lingual, sexual, occupational, and family attributes; consider how narrow your experience with your one sex, one race, one set of parents and siblings, one or a few spouses, none to a few children, and so on. Each soul represents a larger theme focused with laserlike precision into a specific arena offering a unique crucible for learning and growth.

The experiences you have from birth onward further narrow the range of potential. Whether your parents are loving, harsh, or indifferent; whether you have siblings and how you relate to them; the nature of your schooling; your ability to get along with others; the person you choose to marry; your children (with their disparate life themes not always congruent with yours!); your occupational choice, and so forth, all represent slender strands of potential pulled into actualization from the vast sea of probabilities in which you swim. Even given the same parents, economic status, and early childhood experiences, imagine how many different ways your life could play itself out; how many choices you have made to reach today, while other paths were not taken.

Here is where we come to an understanding of what constitutes the inviolate *you* retaining its individual sense of identity throughout eternity. You understand that the physical system operates as a swarm of electromagnetic energy; that your body is itself a grid of fleshed-out electromagnetic patterns which you perceive as the various organs and features; that you operate in the physical system according to the laws of electromagnetism. Out of all the probable variations on your life path swarming about you in pregnant potential, only those *actually pulled into physical manifestation are imprinted in your energy field as electromagnetic "memory."*

In other words, whenever you make a choice and pursue a certain path, the events you draw into physical reality are encoded as electromagnetic information in the swarming energy fields encircling the body. This is where memories are stored, not in the brain. As you grow and age, these electromagnetic memories build up like a library, a private record of every moment of your life. Their combined flavor or tone greatly influences your future, for it is far easier to pull into manifestation events in harmony with your bank of memory than to choose a radically different path. Since probabilities exist as swirling bands of electromagnetic potential, and since like attracts like, a probable event aligned with your body's stored energy patterns is much more likely to be pulled into manifestation than one of highly dissimilar pattern.

So your private library, the record of your life's events, is recorded and maintained in perfect fidelity throughout life. It distinguishes you and your experiences from the far greater probable potentials swirling about you. Upon physical death it serves as the record of your life which remains forever inviolate and unaltered, for it joins the far vaster library of human memory where every life is stored, available for examination.

So is this record, this electromagnetic diary, really you? No. Just as your written autobiography or journals record your life without literally becoming it, so does this electromagnetic autobiography retain its record of your life without the soul's involvement. Who you are today does "live" forever, in the sense that your life's record retains eternal vibrance, but the essential you—the soul—must continue its growth.

Other influences on the soul, beyond a chosen life theme and childhood experience, are more subtle. Chief among these are your reincarnational selves bleeding through with information about their experiences. Since these reincarnational selves are all tied to the same higher self, they will carry the same basic building block of the soul, the same life theme. Each will be born into a different time and place on the linear time continuum as sprouts of potential growing toward mastery of that theme.

Naturally, there will be some exchange between you and your reincarnational selves, sharing as you do bonds to your higher self and a common life purpose. Because bonds between such selves are most often so tenuous and subtle—as tightly focused as you are on each given lifetime—information will be exchanged in the dream state, where the soul's gaze is directed away from earthly life and toward the realm of consciousness.

Like reliving a shared experience with friends or family by telling it over and over, your soul exchanges information with its reincarnational selves as a way of ensuring that balance is maintained within the greater theme; to determine which souls have successfully triumphed over the adversity planted at birth; to learn what works and what doesn't when it comes to successful navigation of the life theme.

The traditional model of reincarnation, as a series of lifetimes planted at intervals along the linear tine continuum, is inadequate for this discussion. For all such reincarnational lives exist "at once" from the perspective of the higher self, outside the space-time framework, and therefore a primitive soul can be planted ahead in linear time of a more evolved soul. The higher self's only intent is to design a cohesive, well-rounded experience of a given theme; thus it plants souls of greater or lesser spiritual evolution scattered along the time continuum. Your next lifetime in linear time might not represent progress at all from the standpoint of who you are today!

Your higher self determines the relative spiritual evolution of each soul by "tuning" the energy fields surrounding and within the body at birth to a specific configuration. This influences the way you think—how evolved, how primitive—and the nature of the events you will most likely attract into manifestation.

Taken together, the soul is composed of a major life theme, a body tuned to think and attract events within a certain range of experience, the record of events carried in electromagnetic vibrance, and communication with reincarnational and probable selves. While the record remains forever *you* within the master library, the essential you—the you who thinks and feels and grows—gradually releases identification with your physical form and climbs into ever greater realms of experience and wisdom.

Reunion and Integration

Once the electromagnetic ledger of a life has been imprinted on the universe, the soul's essence begins the process of reintegration with its higher self. If each life is an offshoot of its higher self, a seed planted in the fertile soil of human experience to sprout, blossom, and wither, then at physical death the essence of consciousness animating that form begins a journey homeward.

Immediately following death comes a period of readjustment, where the thought processes, sensory impressions, and physical manipulation which mark earthly life are gradually released. The facade or camouflage of assuming physical form is not stripped away at once, leaving the soul bewildered and shorn of its familiar modes of absorbing and interpreting information; instead, with the aid of spirit guides the soul is gently eased out of its customary patterns.

Many near-death survivors report visions of tunnels with warm, glowing light beckoning at the far end, reunion with loved ones, and a feeling of intense love and warmth surrounding them at the point of transition. This is all part of the "play" enacted by the soul's spirit guides to ease the transition. There are no tunnels in the nonphysical dimension, needless to say. But the image of a tunnel is a powerful metaphor for the journey awaiting the soul, and the welcome glow at the far end encourages the soul to hasten its release of physical form and the seductive pleasures of earthly life, to move quickly and without conflict toward reintegration.

Reunion with loved ones, if some years have passed since their death, is another comforting fiction offered the departing soul. Since those loved ones have moved on into higher realms of spirit and have lost their identification with the bodies and personalities they wore while in flesh, they cannot "step down" to their earlier form to greet one they loved on earth. But since they left behind an imprint of themselves, and that imprint carries all the happy and intimate memories of time shared with the newly departed soul, a spirit guide aiding the transition can animate an imprint, can hallucinate it into sufficient vibrance and realism that the newly departed soul interprets it as reunion with the loved one.

Gradually the limitations and physical focus of earthly life are sloughed off. This initial period, which lasts anywhere from a few minutes to months or years depending on the soul's attachment to earthly life and willingness to release it, is not the time to review the life and consider its moral balance sheet; that comes later. The initial adjustment period is first experienced as being surrounded by pure, total love and warmth; embraced in a cocoon of unconditional love. This loving sensation, pure and intense, eases the transition for it surpasses the fractured, strings-attached relationships, however loving, most people experience on earth.

As the soul is gently relieved of the facade of physical life, with its dependence on sensory impressions and physical manipulation, the soul comes to accept that it has now released that limited framework and must continue its growth in the realm of pure consciousness. Here it delights in finding that thoughts are transmitted instantly from one to another without the need for symbolic speech or fumbling gestures; communication between two souls is infinitely richer and more vibrant when instantaneous transmission with full fidelity of meaning takes place. So much more material can be transmitted in a given time: the material in a book taking you hours to digest can be readily absorbed in seconds in the realm of pure consciousness.

The Life Review

Once the soul recognizes that release of earthly form means gaining these new and delicious powers, it eagerly embraces growth toward its higher self, its source. Before that reintegration can occur, the soul must review its past life to extract the lessons learned, to tote up the merit badges and demerits accrued, to determine if the world was better or worse off for its participation. This review is always conducted with the counsel of spirit guides of a higher plane than those aiding the transition (who might be considered spiritual midwives as compared to the sagacious insight of the higher guides).

Karma is incurred when intent to cause harm is married to action bringing harm. Both intent and action are necessary to create karma, meaning a bond with another soul who has been harmed by your acts. Merely pondering doing harm to another without following through won't incur karma; accidentally bringing harm without the intent to do so also carries no karmic weight. Intent to do harm plus an act committing harm equals karma. Once karma is incurred, the soul committing the harm and the soul so harmed are bound in a relationship until the karmic bond is released.

The concept of good karma, of performing noble, worthy deeds in order to tilt the scales in favor of your soul's growth, has no validity in the process, for acts committed out of love create no bond, no relationship which must be worked out in the future. Such acts are karmically neutral. While it is comforting to imagine that you and your loved ones will spend eternity together, in truth a loving relationship based on mutual respect and appreciation carries no karmic weight, for no harm has been done. Even in earthly life, true love releases, allows, sets free. Only a relationship carrying negativity must be recast in another shared lifetime.

So the soul's review of its life experiences will look first to how the life theme played itself out—in triumph, defeat, or a simple refusal to effectively deal with the challenges created. On balance, were challenges met head-on and effectively mastered or was the life a series of defeats and increasing despair? If the soul mastered the challenges, triumphed over them, then the particular slice of the master theme played out in that life will be considered resolved by the higher self. If, however, challenges were not surmounted effectively and the life ended with an overall cast of defeat and hopelessness, that particular slice must be recast into another lifetime before it can be reintegrated into the higher self. This does not mean that the same soul must reincarnate; it simply means the higher self sends down another shoot in another place and time but with life circumstances similar to those of the life just released, as another attempt at resolving the challenges to be resolved before reabsorption is possible.

The next step in a life review is to examine its moral balance sheet. On the whole, given that no perfect human being has yet to grace the earth, how do the moral pluses and minuses add up? Were principle and integrity maintained in a world full of seductive expedience and easy compromise? Was love the motive and effect of your actions toward family and others, or did you bring harm? Did you respect the earth and its creatures, or consider them fodder in pursuit of private gain?

Most lifetimes balance on the "good" side of the moral equation, for great compassion and understanding are offered souls releasing earthly life. Human life is a struggle, is meant to be, and this is taken into account. If the moral balance is in the soul's favor, the soul can move on to the next step of its life review. If, however, the soul committed such heinous and brutal acts while in human form that the moral equation is in the negative, meaning that massive karma has been incurred, the process of life review effectively ends as further soul growth cannot occur until the karma is cleared up.

You see, the process is one of gradual release of a specific personality and appearance, and reintegration with the higher self. If a specific personality caused great harm while in human form, then before reintegration can occur that karmic debt must be paid. In this instance, a new offshoot will be created more as a vehicle for the specific personality to "try again" than for the more general purpose of mastering a life theme. The new offshoot will be linked with the imprint left by the soul upon death, for the imprint carries awareness of all relationships, all brutality committed against others. So a new life will be created, and those harmed will frequently be born in relationship to the perpetrator, each such companion also linked to its imprint, so the residue of the past brutality ripples through the new life together.

This is the closest the process comes to the traditional model of reincarnation being a recycling of the same soul from body to body. In the case of great negative karma a new bodily vehicle is prepared and, while it hosts its own soul, that soul is inextricably bound to the imprint left by the perpetrator's life and must work out the karma incurred.

If the life review passes the stages of effective mastery of the life theme and a healthy moral balance, the next step is to review relationships. For this, more than anything, is the crucible of human learning and growth, as well as heartbreak and despair! Relationships are reviewed for their depth of intimacy, whether they were based on respect or derision, whether you "used" people to gratify your own needs or offered them freedom and affirmation.

Since this level of review is above the issue of karmically bound relationships, the issue is not whether great harm was done to others but simply determining the overall flavor or tone of your relationships with others. It is quite possible to sail through life never forming any strong attachments, meaning no karma is incurred, yet such a life is bereft of the richness and growth of a life packed with vibrant relationships.

If there are relationships where love was sullied with jealousy, occasional abuse, or private gratification, frequently those involved will agree to recast themselves together in another lifetime. This is not the same as two karmically bound souls who need to erase the bond between them; instead, it is simply a way for two souls to enrich experience of their life themes by playing different roles at different times and places, like buddies who alternately cherish and antagonize each other as they share adventures.

Reintegration With the Higher Self

Once relationships have been reviewed, the postlife review is complete. At this point the soul, which through the review has retained its sense of itself as a distinct personality and body while on earth, can release this narrow focus and move upward toward reunion and reintegration with the higher self. This idea causes many discomfort, as if they will be "snuffed out" at some point in their spiritual growth, tossed into a melting pot of sundry other souls, there to lose all sense of identity.

We might ask, was it not a healthy step to release the infant's inability to speak and communicate with others? Was it not healthy to release childhood's self-absorption for the worldly concerns of adolescence? Was it not healthy to release fear of the opposite sex to embrace it, to build family upon a sturdy bedrock of love and intimacy? Was it not healthy to release your children in their time, to allow them to begin the family cycle anew? Was it not healthy to release your focus on occupational success, to wind down a bit in old age and savor life's simple pleasures?

Why should the growth stop? Why should a soul wish to forever cling to its sense of itself as one name, one body, in one time and place?

Upon reintegration with the higher self, each life becomes as a day in your life. You look back at the days past, some sublime, some horrific, some uneventful, some cataclysmic; while you agree that each of these days has helped form who you are, you do not cling to them as the sole measure of your identity. So is it with the higher self: your life becomes a day, a flow of moments in the eternal swarm of activity, a unique and precious store of experience held in eternal vibrance.

We can look back and recount our human existences, but we would not wish to identify ourselves with any one body or personality or time period. We call ourselves "we" because all such human incarnations have been fully integrated into who we are; the pronoun "I" is too narrow to hold the fullness of our being. We can "remember" our incarnations because they retain full vitality within our larger gestalt of consciousness, just as you can recall past days. Yet we are so much more than the mere sum of our human incarnations, for we carry those memories into ever greater heights of growth and exploration.

Such is the path awaiting you, friends, upon your release of human life, when the long incarnational cycle is finally completed and the ignorance and awkward groping of a primitive soul have transmuted over millennia to the contemplative wisdom and gentle peace of the enlightened. What is there to fear of death, when it opens the portal through which you soar to such exalted realms?

Cyberspace:
The Manmade Parallel Universe

Technological progress can be understood as the physical manifestation of ideas, processes, and templates emerging into form from the vast unseen realms underlying your experienced reality. That is, anything present on the physical plane exists first as a nonphysical template, an etheric conceptual grid, which can be tapped into by the human mind and brought to form with creativity and tools. Inventions do not spring from the depths of human originality; they are simply "fleshed out" versions of templates floating in eternal viability beyond the reach of your senses. Artists and inventors tap into these banks of potential and, given the limitations of the materials and technology available to them, struggle to replicate in physical form the designs and processes they sense floating in the Great Beyond.

Humanity rides through crests and troughs of accelerating and decelerating vibration as the earth's core energy quickens and slows, married to a deeper universal rhythm. The earth's frequencies delineate the upper and lower reaches of humanity's cultural and spiritual life in a given era, for the templates humanity can pull from its banks of potential carry their own vibrational tone. There must be a basic sympathy of vibration between humanity and the templates it manifests in a given age. This ensures that cultural evolution proceeds at an even, measured pace, and that each evolutionary gain is fully absorbed before the next emerges.

What drives humanity's perpetual quest for technological innovation and fresh art forms? Why not simply be content with the wheel and a box of crayons? The answer is that humanity is driven by the urge to replicate, as closely as possible, the templates and processes governing the unseen realms of consciousness: to create Heaven on Earth. As the earth's vibration accelerates, allowing humanity to reach higher into its banks of potential, technological innovation comes ever closer to physically manifesting the nonphysical universe beneath your experienced reality.

The Global Pool of Consciousness

The physical universe is constructed of many layers of energy and vibration, only the slowest and densest of which are detected by your senses. Your eyes perceive a world of discrete objects separated by empty space. That "empty space" is in fact whirring and buzzing with thick streams of information swirling about the globe at a fierce velocity. One purpose of this revolving blanket of intelligence is to keep you apprised, usually at an unconscious level, of the species' overall condition and experience; and, more specifically, to alert you to events of emotional or physical significance occurring to those you love.

Your thoughts have an electromagnetic reality. These electrical streams flow not only from the brain down the neuronal networks, but also up into the atmosphere. You feed a constant stream of electrically encoded information to the world at large through the crown of your head. This stream is your private contribution to the global swarm of human consciousness. Because you carry a unique energetic "stamp" which identifies you vibrationally as surely as your fingerprint does physically, each unit of encoded information is recognizable as emanating from you and no one else.

Under normal circumstances, these private streams blend into the global pool of consciousness and pass undetected by others. In times of great physical or emotional stress, however, such streams pulse with fierce urgency and power, bursting from the background static of global consciousness to stand out as messages of special urgency. Because such messages carry the stamp of their originator, and because you instantly recognize the messages originating from those you know and love, a stream of urgent importance can trigger conscious feelings of concern for loved ones who may be half a world away. Reports are legion of those inexplicably gripped with sudden concern for loved ones, only to discover later that at the moment of sensed urgency the loved one had suffered great injury or died.

This is a natural and intended result of setting up the physical system in a way that ensures privacy of thought while allowing enough sensitivity to remote events that suffering and death are telepathically communicated to loved ones. The purpose of a camouflage physical system such as yours is that thoughts must be communicated through symbolic speech or gesture rather than directly, mind to mind. Nonetheless, each person is plugged into the global communication network and can, if receiving distress signals from loved ones, consciously detect their anguish.

From Camel to Cyberspace

As long as human tribes have needed to communicate with others out of their immediate vicinity, a set of agreed-upon symbols to carry their messages and a means of transportation to deliver them have been required. Driven by the natural desire that such symbolic messages be clear and detailed, and that they arrive as quickly as possible, two primary focuses of human technological progress have been the development of sophisticated language systems and faster modes of transportation. Subconsciously driving these efforts has been the urge to physically replicate the vibrational communication system encircling the globe, which carries richly detailed energetic messages around the world in mere moments.

For most of its history, humanity's transportation systems have evolved slowly: from runners carrying messages on foot, to employing beasts of burden or the wheel, to sending missives by ship or railroad. It is only in the last century or so that rapid progress has been made in devising new, more rapid methods of communication. The telegraph is one, allowing almost instantaneous transmission of messages, coded in a specially devised language. The telephone represents the next great leap, and to this day it remains the most authentic mode of communication, for it directly carries the voice with all its emotional nuances rather than reducing language to written symbol. The fitful development of a telephone carrying video images represents a leap into still greater fidelity of transmission, for it offers the rich embellishment of facial expressions and gestures.

At the same time, those who prefer to communicate through written correspondence find that the days of the Pony Express and steamboat have thankfully passed, and letters can now cross the country in days or even overnight. Those willing to sacrifice aesthetics for expedience can transmit written symbols instantaneously via facsimile machines.

Communicating through cyberspace represents a quantum leap of an altogether different nature than the gradual refinements in language and transportation which enhanced the complexity, and shortened the delivery time, of communication through the centuries. For moving into the digital age carries with it a fundamental shift in the way information is organized and disseminated. Until now, the race's accumulated knowledge has been collected and organized by writers, printed in media such as books, magazines, and newspapers, and made available to those with the means to acquire it. The process is a *mechanical* one, requiring paper, typesetting, and transportation to make information available.

The move into the digital age marks a shift from a mechanical communication system to an *energetic* system in which information is created, disseminated and retrieved without ever being reduced to paper and physically transported. This represents a great leap in sophistication, for it much more closely replicates the world's "original" communication system, the vast vibrational network encircling the globe.

One striking feature of cyberspace communication, which makes it such a leap above all other means of exchange, is that sender and recipient no longer need a physical address. The postal service delivers mail to a specific domicile; the telephone company rings a phone number in only one location. Others depend on your being consistently available at regular times and places in order to communicate with you.

Cyberspace communication eliminates the need for a physical address. Instead, once one has a "virtual" address, others can send messages from anywhere, at any time, with the confidence that the message will find its intended recipient, wherever he or she may be. That recipient may be anywhere in the world, but with a computer and telephone line (and possibly a satellite), messages can be retrieved instantly. No paper, no transportation. Communicating via cyberspace eliminates the need to inscribe messages on paper and pay to have them transported to a physical address. This represents a great leap closer to replicating the energetic communication system surrounding the globe.

The Binary Universe

There is another highly significant aspect of the evolution from physical means of communication to energetic means.

The digital revolution marks the transition into an era when various media—language, photography, music, video—can be reduced to binary form, stored and reproduced with perfect fidelity, and transmitted across the vast reaches of cyberspace in moments. All such media are founded on the computer's binary system which, at its most elemental level, reduces information to a series of on/off values, pulsing in elaborate sequences to build complex tapestries of information.

This is how the physical universe works as well: a steady pulsation between the physical and nonphysical realms transmits information across the vibrational divide. The physical universe blinks "on" and "off" as it rides this primal pulsation. A thrust of energy and structural information bursts from the nonphysical realms to organize a coherent physical universe: this is the "on" pulsation. The physical realm then transmits responsive information as to its condition and unfolding events: this is the "off" pulsation *during which physical reality ceases to exist.* Your mind unconsciously leaps the gap of non-existence, for the pulsation is far too rapid for your senses to detect. You live in the illusion of a physical world when, for 12 hours out of every 24, that world does not exist.

Thus the universe operates as a binary system, rooted to a primal on/off pulsation carrying information across the vibrational barrier between physical and nonphysical realms. It is no accident that computers should use the same basic system to store and handle information; as is always the case, technology edges ever closer to replicating the deeper structures and processes on which the universe is based. Each such innovative advance brings you one step closer to physically re-creating the deeper universal system, toward manifesting "heaven on earth."

Cyberchips and Satellites:
The Next Great Leap

For all the wondrous improvements in communication brought about by the computer revolution and creation of cyberspace, there remain several impediments to physical re-creation of the global energetic communication system. The most obvious is that expensive and sophisticated machines are required to communicate via cyberspace. This limits use of the technology to businesses and affluent individuals (and the average First World denizen is affluent by world standards).

The second impediment is that dependence on physical structures and systems (such as telephone lines) limits access to cyberspace; one cannot retrieve e-mail from remote jungles or floating on the high seas without at least a sophisticated satellite hookup (which further increases the expense and limits access).

Because your race is driven to replicate the global communication system, and because that system allows instantaneous, unimpeded communication with all other individuals, technological innovation will forge ahead in the direction of reducing cost and increasing availability of access. This will take several forms. The first is that computers, or at least their communication systems, will be reduced in size to a tiny implant (a "cyberchip") which can be burrowed under the skin. A system of satellites sweeping the global skies will transmit messages from anywhere in the world to the cyberchip carried by a target individual. This eliminates the need to lug a laptop about the globe and find a functional telephone line.

Initially, the cyberchip will emit an audible or visual signal indicating that information awaits retrieval; the recipient will then have to access a traditional computer node to retrieve messages. As the technology is further refined, the implant will itself transmit information through coupling with a pager-size translation device carried in one's pocket. When held against the skin above the implant, a sensor on the translation device will read the binary flow and translate it either into written words or audible speech. Thus, with only a solar-powered device the size of a pager one can be in unbroken communication with the entire planet, however remote one's location.

For all the progress this level of innovation represents, it still depends on physical devices which can be damaged or lost, abruptly cutting off cyber-communication. The next great technological leap—and this lies beyond the lifetime of most now living—will be to place the implants under the scalp or in the brain, where they translate the brain's electrical activity into binary pulsations which can be broadcast to others. Just as each living being has a unique vibrational "stamp" which identifies it as the source of its energetic messages, so will each chip have a unique code allowing identification of the source of brain-to-brain communication.

Here is an example of how such a system might work. Employing voice-recognition technology, one could announce, "Message to Mom." The phrase "message to" alerts the cyberchip that it is to begin taking dictation. "Mom" tells it to whom it should send the message. The text of the message would be spoken aloud; the cyberchip would read the neuronal pulsations translating thought to spoken language and convert the neurological patterns to binary pulsations.

When the speaker announces, "End of message," the chip ceases taking dictation. It then transmits the binary stream skyward, to the waiting satellites encircling the globe, which beam the message down to the uniquely encoded chip worn by Mom. She can then "play" the message by having her chip translate the binary pulsations back to neuronal pulsations, allowing her to hear her beloved son or daughter wishing her Happy Binary Birthday in the privacy of her head.

A Brave New Cyberworld?

Lest it sound as if we are endorsing an Orwellian night-
mare of remote-controlled zombies, let us look at the broader
picture of which technological innovation is one part. As
mentioned, the earth rides through waves of rising and slowing vibration, and the earth's vibration in a given era determines the upper and lower reaches of human culture. As a
rule, healthy cultures ride the twin tracks of technology and
spirituality, with growth in either aspect reinforced by similar
progress in the other. Technology is itself morally neutral;
questions as to the morality and appropriateness of its use lie
in the realm of ethics, values, and spiritual wisdom. A healthy
culture, whose technology and spirituality progress evenly,
will always reach consensus as to the appropriate use of technological innovation.

The crisis in your day is that technology races forward
unchecked by spiritual wisdom. Spiritual life remains rooted
in the millennia-old dogma of the Judeo-Christian faith, an
appropriate worldview for the Dark and Middle Ages, but
woefully inadequate for the Space Age. As a result, science has
divorced itself completely from spiritual life—has rejected
God and his wondrous seven days in favor of the Big Bang—
and staggers about in hazy amorality, creating both marvels
and horrors with equal zeal. Bereft of a sturdy spiritual compass, science has lost the ethical and moral wisdom to evaluate
the appropriateness of its creations.

Because technological progress rides atop the earth's accelerating vibration, and because that acceleration stimulates
spiritual growth as well, by the time such devices as cyberchips have evolved your spiritual life will have similarly
evolved, reducing the potential for their more nefarious uses.
Western spiritual life is in a state of great turmoil in your day
as the old religious order—grounded in separatism and a paternal sky god—grinds against the new spiritual order founded

on holism and divinity immanent in all beings. Assuming humanity emerges from the struggle with a new spiritual order firmly established, the darker potentials of cyberchips, or any technology, will remain unrealized.

The darkest potential uses of such technology lie, of course, with government. For governments always seek control over their peoples, even governments pledging allegiance to free speech and democracy. Because the free flow of *information* is one of the greatest threats to any government's control, government insists on regulating the transmission of information. Television and radio stations must be approved and licensed; "rogue" operators transmitting clandestine radio signals are hunted down and jailed. Any published threat to overthrow the government is labeled treason and is punishable by death.

Governments are rarely run by visionaries riding the cutting edge of innovation; thus the irrepressible urge to escape government repression and freely exchange information is aided by technology's ceaseless evolution. Today governments worldwide are bewildered as they face the unruly anarchy of the Internet. Who owns it, who runs it, where are the levers of control? No one knows; it is everywhere and nowhere; it has more of a virtual than a physical reality. The free and unimpeded global transmission of information is deeply unsettling to government, and the times ahead will see increasing efforts to rein in and regulate the Internet. Such an affront to government control of information cannot be permitted to stand.

Ultimately, such efforts will fail as bureaucrats are no match for the wit and cunning of cyber-visionaries forging end runs around government interference. One of the trends in the larger cultural transition is the diminution of powerful federal governments in favor of smaller, more localized rule. This trend is accelerated as more and more people log onto cyberspace and escape government control of their access to information. This battle can be expected to intensify in the times ahead, with free speech ultimately triumphing over government repression.

As we have described, the current revolution in communicating via cyberspace is one step in the greater process of physically replicating the vast energetic communication system encircling the globe. What lies ahead are reducing dependence on machinery to transmit and receive information, miniaturizing broadcast technology, expanding access from the wealthy to all, and fighting government control and censorship of cyberspace. Beyond the upcoming decades of technological innovation and social debate lies a new era of instantaneous communication, free of censorship or repression, allowing every individual to travel freely while maintaining immediate contact with their business and family circles. This is the promise of the cyberspace revolution.